UNBUTTONED
Who Says Men Can't Change?

Ken Fink

Transformational Publishing, Inc.
1973 Beach Avenue
Atlantic Beach, FL 32233

Fink, Kenneth N.
    Unbuttoned – Who Says Men Can't Change?

Layout: J. L. Saloff
Cover Design: Mary Fisher Designs
Fonts: Hoefler Text; Lydian MT; Humana Serif

ISBN: 9780972739-0-8
Copyright information available upon request

First Edition

Printed on acid-free paper in the United States of America

Dedication

This book is dedicated to the teachers, friends, healers, fellow-travelers and family who, during my journey, supported my path without judgment and, by the way they led their own lives, demonstrated the power of personal discovery. These contributors, many of whom are written about in this book, taught me that a wider variety of choices was permissible and that there were many different realities to choose from, which both expanded and enriched my view of life. It is also dedicated as an encouragement to those who wish to make their own journey into self-discovery in their own way.

Unbuttoned / Ken Fink

TABLE OF CONTENTS

INTRODUCTION

by Nancy Slonim Aronie

Unbuttoned / Ken Fink

*I*f you have a brother, a boyfriend, a husband , a father, or simply a male friend, *Unbuttoned* is a must read. From the first sentence to the last line, Ken Fink takes you on his soul's journey to dispel the myth of what a "good man" should be. Without a role model for feelings but recognizing that life is a classroom, Mr. Fink shares his compelling story of a man/lawyer lost in the corporate world searching to find meaning without losing but redefining power.

In this beautifully sensitive book, filled with parables and personal vignettes, Ken Fink provides a map straight into the heart. For men who are wondering why their lives are filled with stress, broken relationships and loneliness, *Unbuttoned* is a necessary Bible. He admits that he still has an inclination to be reactive (masculine) rather than responsive (feminine) but after years of meeting with healers and spiritual teachers and deepening his practice as a human being he knows now that there is a higher consciousness available to him. That consciousness is available to everyone, he says. Sometimes you have to find it through trauma as he did. His type A personality still rears its ugly head ever so often, but he has learned how to take time out for himself and find balance, a word that was not even in his former vocabulary. He shares his new interests like West African drumming, which he found helped raise his energy which he had lost during his illness.

Once he found his new way of being, it affected all areas of his life. Now his relationship with his children is more full, more real, and more loving. He has a new appreciation of the divine and a new reverence in his acknowledgement of God.

In *Unbuttoned*, the author never preaches, but just lets us in on his own transformational process—never the expert, always the student. *Unbuttoned* is a wild and powerful trip that takes the reader from the boardroom to the ashram. I recommend Reader, that you make your reservation at once!

Nancy Slonim Aronie, author
Writing from the Heart
Hyperion Press

PREFACE

"Most men lead lives of quiet desperation."
HENRY DAVID THOREAU

Unbuttoned / Ken Fink

*M*y experience was one of desperation. But there was nothing quiet about it.

I had been brought up in a male-oriented middle class culture. Like many men, I was expected to maintain a continuously high standard of achievement. In my particular family those achievements were in the form of academic, athletic and organizational honors. I had a great record of accomplishments in these areas as both a young and a presumably mature adult. Obstacles were simply an invitation to train harder or study longer. If I had to, I would deny myself experiences I now see as essential to well-being. Instead, I was expected to constantly focus on my goals – no pain, no gain drove all of us chasing success, status, the good life.

I had received, as expected, one honor after another. Among them: in high school, president of my fraternity, a member of the tennis team and a member of the national honor society. In college, president of my fraternity, appointment to the men's judiciary and graduation with honors from an Ivy League business school. This continued into law school, where I became a law review editor. By the time I graduated I was considered a valuable commodity and basically could choose to work with almost any law firm in the country. And so I was wined and dined by lawyer suitors and then hired by the best of them.

This outer success continued into my work life. I quickly became a partner in a prestigious law firm in my hometown of Jacksonville,

Florida, and served on several boards of directors. You accurately could have described me as "a young man on the rise."

But my life was far from fulfilling. While outwardly it seemed a perfect existence – career success, community status, a lovely wife, three terrific kids and an impressive house in a prime neighborhood – I felt empty, restless and on automatic. Who was I, really, I occasionally asked myself? At other times, in rare moments of self-reflection, I wondered what it might be like to feel peaceful and content and to step beyond the box of my life. But the work was so demanding, the responsibilities so overwhelming, and the home life so intense, that I found myself running from one commitment to another like a wind-up action doll.

Many people lived that unrelenting, hectic way at that time and still do. When asked, they usually say they have no choice. And so most of their lives are spent on the run. No value is given to just being, or for time spent in personal reflection, and so those essential pieces of a balanced life are rarely built into it.

After I had worked four years, day and night, to achieve partnership in record-breaking time, I couldn't understand why that success left me with a profound sense of emptiness. After eleven additional years of successful legal practice, I recall sitting at my desk wondering if I could spend the rest of my life at this breakneck pace, and if I could, who was I really doing it for? Things could have continued in a mindless chase after some illusory fulfillment if the great mystery of life hadn't intruded in a totally unpredictable and jolting way.

All the things I had devoted my life to began to crack. My sixteen-year marriage had come apart; I suddenly became ill with an undiagnosed disorder; and I was forced to leave my profession. Soon after, I found myself drawn into a world of alternative lifestyles and spending time with people motivated more by their inner longings and less by ambition for outer achievements. An observer might have called this just a mid-life crisis, since I was forty years old and desperately seeking to change my entire life. Though it took me a while to grasp what was happening, eventually I saw clearly that, in fact, I had embarked on a path of personal transformation.

Like others I've met along the way, I felt I had no choice. I now see there are two possibilities when life shakes us up in these ways. Driven by an insistent impulse for change, we can either choose to take a hard look at everything we've held sacred or become helplessly caught in a whirlwind of painful events demanding changes and upheavals that seem not of our own choosing. This call to transformation, if not met consciously, usually begins with a crisis – an illness, a problematic relationship, a calamity with money, an overwhelming urge to get away from it all. For me, the changes that followed started with the need to get my health, physical and emotional, functional again and then inexorably led to a quest for greater meaning. I would be asking, for the first time, "Who am I?" and "What is my purpose?", questions I never felt I had the luxury to raise.

Not surprisingly, I received little permission or support from many of the people I knew for what was to become an adventure into inner space and would change my entire outer circumstances. I should add that mine was specifically a man's journey, with challenges often different from what most women experience on their quests, although the two paths also have much in common.

Where I came from men were expected to be breadwinners first and foremost, and secondly to provide protection and security for those around them. There was an absolute taboo against expressing most emotions, which were considered signs of weakness. In particular, we feared that an emotional expression or outburst in the workplace could spell professional death. I, along with the other men I knew, rarely stepped back to reflect on our lives. If we deviated from the prescribed path we could expect to be attacked and belittled, often by those who would have to assume more responsibility if we dared to question the excessive obligations we had taken on. We could also expect contempt from those who would never consider taking time out to scrutinize their choices, their goals, their lifestyles, or themselves. If I were to discover that there was something more or different, it could challenge the comfortable assumptions of those around me going full tilt ahead. For a man to go looking for a radical life change, inner and outer, with no tangible goal, was heretical, laughable and definitely not masculine.

In spite of these considerable deterrents, I was not to be deterred. I quickly found that my new world could offer exciting and previously unknown possibilities, for myself personally and for my contribution to others. I also learned, to my surprise, that if I stayed conscious and paid attention, I would be guided each step of the way.

And so, in 1985 I set out on a journey from which there could be no turning back. It would be a challenging, life-altering odyssey, often hard, sometimes thrilling, and unequivocally necessary. Ultimately it would be my true birthing into life.

This book is the story of my seventeen-plus years on that journey. It's about the amazing people I met and the deep and sometimes wild experiences lived along the way. I have also tried to communicate what I understand to be the lessons and insights gained from each leg of the trip, as this is the essence of it all.

It is written with the intention of encouraging those on their own journeys, and with the hope that others reading it who feel trapped and a need to explore will find here some guidance and inspiration to free themselves in their own way. And it is written especially for men who, like me, bought into a myth of what a "good man" should be and who have had no model, and probably little permission or support, to find out for themselves who they really are and what their lives might be if guided by their own wisdom and hearts.

Ken Fink

Unbuttoned / Ken Fink

Chapter One

A GLIMPSE OF THE FUTURE

"The only people always rushing around are those
who don't know where they are going."
GUDNI GUNNARSSON, Life Coach

Unbuttoned / Ken Fink

When I walked out of a legal seminar and raced to a nearby mountain town, I got my first taste of a new kind of freedom.

It was the late 70s; I was in my mid-thirties, and I had traveled from my home in Florida to attend a securities law symposium at the University of Colorado in Boulder. I started the day in a coat and tie, and my intentions were appropriately serious. I was to attend a week-long workshop with a couple of hundred people, mostly men. My purpose was to learn the latest legal developments in corporate and securities law. I was charged with the responsibility of reporting developments to my law firm, where I was then a junior partner.

As the day progressed, the atmosphere in the auditorium became overly oppressive to me; I began to hear the mountains calling my name. During the break, I realized I couldn't return to the seminar. I grabbed my briefcase, hopped in my rental car and, with a map in hand, headed out of the city. It was a beautiful summer day. As I drove up the famous Boulder Canyon, I could see waterfalls cascading on both sides of the road. Crowds gathered to watch climbers scale the sheer cliffs. I rolled down all four windows to listen to the sound of running water from the stream to my left. With so many panoramas to view, it was difficult to keep my eyes on the road. The pristine nature of the surroundings left me feeling unexpectedly unburdened, and I felt exhilarated that I had deviated from the expected and taken the day for myself.

Debra, a friend from home, had once told me that she had lived in a nearby mountain town called Gold Hill with a fellow named Hugh while she was in college. I thought that might be a good place to start my adventure. I drove along the Boulder Canyon road for several miles until I came upon a wooden sign which read, "Gold Hill – 11 miles." The road twisted and turned at first and then slowly narrowed as I ascended from Boulder at 5,400 feet above sea level toward Gold Hill at 8,500 feet. The last five miles were on an unpaved dirt road.

I stopped the car several times to step outside, where I was greeted by the unfamiliar but very sweet sounds of the mountains. The higher I went, the more I noticed the contrast between the living sounds around me and the harsh and mechanical noises of the city below.

When I arrived in Gold Hill, everybody I asked seemed to know Hugh but I was told that he was out of town for a few days.

Weary from the constant busyness of my life, it was a relief to simply park myself in a local coffee house, where I remained for several hours. I soon found myself feeling hypnotized by the slow, ambling pace of the town. In marked contrast to my life at home and my corporate and securities law practice, where I was continually facing deadlines and running from one place to another, here in Gold Hill people seemed free of that kind of intensity. Once a woman behind the counter at the fried chicken place across the street from my law office asked me why I was always running. It startled me that this stranger would notice my pace. It was even more surprising that it struck her as out of the ordinary. I silently denied any validity to her observation. I wasn't ready to look at anything about my life that might challenge its insanity.

The morning in Gold Hill did not seem like the kind of Tuesday I was used to. People were relaxed and stopped to say hello and visit with each other. What I found most startling was that these leisurely people included men and not just an isolated male wandering through town. Moreover, although these men appeared able-bodied and functional, they also seemed friendly, happy and in no hurry to get anywhere.

This was not my everyday reality. Where I came from men's time was accounted for by the hour. In fact, in my law practice, we accounted for our time by as little as one tenth of an hour and billed clients according to the totals of these minuscule increments of time. The men I knew might plan some recreation for the weekend – maybe a pickup football game or golf – but even there the interactions were often competitive, tough and fast.

Among my co-workers one suit said hello to the next only on the way down the long corridors, usually in a hurry. We talked the language of our business and directed the substance of our conversations carefully, often in ways calculated to sound our own horns and advance our positions within the firm. We rarely spoke of the important personal matters in our lives and especially not those things that were troubling us. In fact, we were hesitant to reveal any truth that might make us vulnerable for fear that someone would take advantage of it. When I returned to the seminar the next day my mind, like that of the fictional Walter Mitty, fantasized about the delicious little mountain town while the lecturer droned on. I asked myself whether life could ever slow to a point when enjoying the moment was an option. I looked out at the mountains but the little town had disappeared and its memory seemed elusive, like the lost gold of Eldorado.

On the Friday night before my Saturday departure, the phone rang in my hotel room. The caller, identifying himself as Hugh, led the conversation by saying he was sorry to have missed me. I was expecting a perfunctory, "Please tell Debra hello," when, instead, he invited me to visit the next day. "I'll get some food and we can cook out," he announced. I was startled and touched by the generosity of his offer to spend the day with a stranger. Uncharacteristically, I decided to postpone my return for another day.

Hugh's house sat at the top of the hill at one end of this one-street town. There, we cooked hamburgers, talked to the friends who stopped by and that evening walked down to the well-known Gold Hill Inn. Most of the people who lived in Gold Hill skipped the Inn's five-star restaurant but gathered, instead, nightly at the bar to listen to music and just be together. I loved the feeling of the small town camaraderie.

Hugh, who had been a writer in college, was then writing a history of silver mining in Colorado. He took me for a long walk around the town, showing me the historical sights. Along the way he pointed to a place at a higher elevation where the train used to run and told me how, in the old days, his college friends would build a fire and wait for hours for the train to pass through.

At the old cemetery, stopping to read the tombstones, I tried to imagine the lives of the people who had filled the space between the dates of birth and death. Where family members were buried near each other and family trees were etched into the stones, I recreated their lives in my imagination. Was the woman to the right his first wife and the woman to the left his second, and if so, did they resent sharing the husband in death or did they share him in life as well? What caused the premature death of so many people, I wondered, and in those days what was considered premature? I could sense the heavy toll exacted by the hardships that had occurred in this hard-living town high in the glorious but unforgiving Rockies. Only later did I realize how rare it was for me to give my curiosity and imagination full rein and how pleasurable it was for me that day.

With Hugh I experienced a degree of openness and casualness that I had not known for a very long time. I was returning home the next day and my heart yearned for more days like this one. But that seemed an impossibility. I had a wife and three children, substantial bills to pay and a long list of tasks needing my attention. In the face of a life that was competitive and demanding, the kind of exploration I had just had a taste of was a luxury out of the question. I even feared that in taking this week off I was losing a competitive advantage.

Almost a decade had passed since my trip to Gold Hill when I awoke one morning and found to my great surprise that I was unable to get out of my bed. I lay there feeling flu-like, with glands swollen under my arms, in my neck and in my groin. I tried to get up, but it was futile. I gazed numbly at the ceiling. It was unusual for me to be sick. But even after several days in bed I was no better.

My illness had come on suddenly. Yesterday I could run ten miles, and today I could not stand up. I was totally debilitated, and the swollen glands in my neck, under my arms and in my groin were painful, sometimes feeling as though I'd been suddenly stung by a wasp.

As much in pain as my body was, the illness was more devastating mentally for me, for nothing I did seemed to make any difference. I knew I would be better tomorrow – doesn't the body heal itself naturally? – but each tomorrow I was unimproved. It was like being in the marshes; I could neither move in any direction nor see dry land anywhere. I feared that if I remained in this place the mud would eventually sink beneath my feet like quicksand. I felt enraged and helpless, both of these feelings very new to my awareness. My frustration was exacerbated by anger. I wanted to take a knife and excise the troublesome lumps, yet I knew the swollen glands signaled that my immune system was fighting some invader and thus they could be considered uncomfortable friends. Instead of awakening each morning to coffee and the newspaper, the first thing I now did was to palpate the glands under my arms to see if they had returned to normal. This self-examination resulted in daily disappointment, as the swollen glands never got smaller. Sometimes the swelling would leave one side of my body, and I'd experience a short-term elation only to find that it had stealthily moved to the other side.

I had considered myself a busy man, but now I could not move. My mind said, "Let's go," but my body said, "No way, buster." I remained watchful, believing that sooner or later I would outsmart the invader, but my attentiveness made utterly no difference. I had thought, when I was a young child, that as long as I stayed aware of my breathing I would never die, but that same hypervigilance now was useless.

As difficult as the swollen glands were, the fatigue was crippling. At first I had thought I would return to work in a day or two. My mind sought to gain control over the recalcitrant body and my bravado kept reminding me that I was a partner in a prestigious law firm. This kind of thing didn't happen to that kind of person. I telephoned the firm's managing partner each morning to report that I expected to return the following day, only to be embarrassingly forced to call again in the afternoon to report that I had not improved.

My firm insisted, and prided itself, on always accommodating the client's needs and meeting its timetable regardless of any personal sacrifice, always willing to outwork our legal competitors. We would gallantly push through no matter what. In spite of the fact that I had contracted some unnamed and very persistent malady – the doctors could say only that it was probably viral – I felt I had no excuse for not getting on with my life. As sick as I was, still I felt ashamed of my condition. Finally I asked for a several months leave of absence to pull myself together, although I had no clue how that might happen or what it would look like. Over time, I learned that my body had rebelled so violently in reaction to the way I had been living my life. This violence to the body would ultimately become the force that would thrust me permanently, without conscious volition on my part, out of the legal and business world.

At this time I had been divorced for almost a year following a difficult two year separation. Since I was now required to contribute to the support of two households, the financial pressure on me had grown substantially. I was also deeply saddened by the physical separation from my children. And so, I was in considerable anguish – physically in great pain, emotionally devastated by the losses and changes in my personal life, mentally at a loss for understanding and direction, economically on the edge, and of course but unknown to me at the time, spiritually bankrupt.

To name this a typical male mid-life crisis would be to demean the true nature of the crisis, which I would come to see as a clear call to awakening into wholeness. What was happening to me and to other men I've met along the path could not be remedied by a new car or a young babe, the usual media portrayal of mid-life male angst. It could only be met by a deep and often radical redirection of one's life.

I had no awareness at that time that my leave of absence would be the beginning of an odyssey that would take me into worlds previously unknown. Instead of gathering more achievements and accomplishments, I would venture into a world of alternative realities that would include yogis, ashrams, clairvoyants and psychic surgeons. I would be interacting with healers and counselors of all varieties, some with national reputations and others unknown to the public and living in unmarked houses down roads I previously had not dared to travel. The notion of what was real had begun to change for me. Experiences of alternate realities now competed with the beliefs about the material world which I had mastered through my formal education, fifteen years of law practice and an adulthood characterized by personal, family and civic responsibility. My clients were sophisticated and well-traveled, and their problems dealt with the nuances and intricacies of the business and financial world, corporate mergers, public financings and business reorganizations. But all of this training and experience had little value for the everyday issues I was now facing. When help finally arrived it was from the alternative world that had been non-existent for me until I took up part-time residence there, and not from those – friends, family, professionals – who had filled my life until then.

Chapter Two

A NEW BEGINNING:
First Steps

"A journey of 1,000 miles begins with one step."
LAO-TZU, Tao Te Ching

Unbuttoned / Ken Fink

*W*hen I took the first step out of my "normal," everyday routines, I had no intention beyond getting on with my life as it had been. I knew my objectives. I intended to reach them by getting back into the same saddle, which was the only saddle I knew. I wanted to heal, return to work, get beyond the pain of my recent divorce and do my part to raise my children.

I felt it would be only a short time before I recovered and that my leave of absence was only a temporary detour from the path I knew so well. I believed doggedness alone would carry me, as it had through so many years of effort, discipline and achievement.

My first order of business was to heal my body. I didn't have the foggiest idea of how to go about that. I had always relied on traditional medicine, as had my family, but the doctors I consulted were of no help. After many weeks and various tests, the specialist concluded that an extremely high Epstein-Barr reading was at the root of my illness. It was then theorized that the Epstein-Barr virus was a cause of mononucleosis, but my doctors were reluctant to name my condition chronic mononucleosis, a disease neither acknowledged nor understood at that time. I was told that regretfully there was no known treatment for the virus and symptoms I was manifesting, which essentially closed the door to traditional medicine for me.

At the same time, my emotional life was in turmoil. Mental health counselors told me I was suffering from anxiety and depression. And so none of the things that had once promised happiness and well-being—

a traditional marriage, a good job, the medical and mental health professions—now seemed relevant or of any use to my situation.

My personal seeking had actually begun long before my illness. On nights when my ex-wife had her bridge gathering at our house, I drove to nearby St. Augustine to hang out in a neighborhood bar and mingle with people quite unlike those I encountered in my everyday life. They were shrimpers, bikers, tourists, artists and blue-collar workers. Without a briefcase, white shirt or dictating machine – the symbols of my so-called status – I could see reflected back to me who I was beyond my roles and personal story.

Once people heard what I did for a living, though, the conversation would become less personal and they less frank and available, as though I held some power over them. The men then tended to tell me long-winded stories of their or their family's history with lawyers. Women would perk up; I read this as a sign that they concluded this guy was smart and had money, and I saw that status alone could trigger sexual availability. I found these forays into self-exploration to be engaging; I learned more in these environments about myself than when I interacted with an exclusively homogenous group.

I had lived what many considered to be the idyllic life. My house, which I had personally chosen, was a large colonial fronted with white columns and located in a fashionable neighborhood. The mention of the law firm in which I was now a partner bestowed upon me instantaneous credibility and an automatic place at the table. I had a promising economic future and an active social life. What more could I want?

It did not occur to me to notice that I had become a Ken "doing," a wind-up action figure running from one place to another without thought about where I was going. I had neither the time nor the inclination for introspection. I was consumed by putting out today's fire, and it took me years to realize that these fires were often started and fanned by others for their own objectives—and had been consuming my own life force.

I was living the female fantasy of a knight on a white horse, a pretense of perfection and impossible protection. There was no space for me to consider whether or not I was satisfied; I simply couldn't afford to uncover the extent of my unconsciousness and exhaustion. The mere suggestion that I might be considering a different life direction would naturally strike fear into the hearts of those who depended on me. I felt like a workhorse with little backup.

At the same time I was becoming aware of my lack of personal time for myself, my marriage had stopped providing the haven I expected and needed it to be. My wife and I had been childhood sweethearts for many years and had been married for seven years when complications from outside the marriage took over. In many ways we were never again a couple.

It was hard to believe at the time, but ultimately I would recognize a silver lining in this cloud of anguish. It would set me free at a time my soul seemed to require that.

We tried to rescue the marriage through intensive counseling, but that failed. Eventually I had the choice of either leaving her and my children or continuing in a situation intolerable for both of us and unlikely to change.

I felt our connection shatter after a night of true revelation. I knew instantly that the foundation of our partnership had been broken. In fact, I heard a sharp snap, as if a plastic ruler had been broken, the two distinct parts no longer even connected by loose strands. There could be no mending of this fracture, which soon turned into a mangled break. I had never seriously thought about divorce or separation—it had not been in my family tradition. Now I needed to face the fact that my marriage was over, pull myself together and gather the strength to move on. I knew I was the one who would have to make the move.

Still, I had trouble breaking free. While we went through the motions of working on our relationship, its remnants over the next six months spiraled downward like a plane in freefall. One day I saw a poster on a friend's wall that said, simply, "If you can't change the winds, then set your sail." I moved out several days later, at age 38, after fourteen years of marriage. I moved to a nearby beach community for the period we called a "trial separation," but I knew in my heart, as I drove my carload of possessions out of the family home, that I would never go back. There was never an attempted reconciliation on either side, the time for this marriage had passed. While the aftermath remained difficult for years, the product of this union, three children conceived in love, remained an enduring blessing for which I am ever grateful and which measured this union at its best.

My wife soon met a man different from those she had known before. He was kind, deeply religious, and seemed to be satisfied with work, religion, and home life. She remarried within a year of our divorce and he moved into my former house. His stabilizing influence helped through the aftermath of this rocky process and was a blessing to all of us. Without it, the impact of the divorce upon the children might have been worse. My son and two daughters, then at the vulnerable ages of five, eight, and eleven paid a price nonetheless, although I believe children who have gone through a divorce process give up the fairytale illusions of life and are more likely to work harder to make their own relationships work.

After a divorce most parties move towards the changes they needed to make while they were married. For me, it was slowing down and finding more time to spend with my children, in contrast to my previous work-focused hectic life. This evolved over time and I became a better parent, including soccer Dad, Indian Guide Chief, running races with my oldest daughter, but mostly just sitting quietly with the children in their normal activities. Some of my energy formerly consumed in the divorce process was now available for me and my children. During the following years their mother did the hard day to day work of their upbringing, was present attentively when they needed her, furnished the emotional framework in which they were raised and provided the roots of a stable home life with extended family functions in which they were nourished. In the process, I was freed to take my journey, which involved a more mobile lifestyle than otherwise would have been available and gave birth to the adventurer within.

Within a year of the divorce, my mother was diagnosed with colon cancer. After her operation, we—my brother and I—were told her surgeons had not been able to "get it all." This was a devastating blow to me. My mother and her mother, my dear grandmother who lived with her at the time, were my closest family.

Since my father had died and my brother and his family lived in Atlanta, I would have to be the center of my mother's support through her illness. I assumed this responsibility over time but was not ready for it then, as I was still in the early stage of my illness and very depleted; I barely had enough energy to care for myself.

Since my body remained unresponsive to whatever I tried in order to get well, and there was tremendous pressure to get well, I began to consider looking for other routes back to health. And so I decided to seek the advice of my good friend Lucy, who had a high level of consciousness and a strong orientation toward healing. She had been my massage therapist and also a yoga teacher; most importantly, I really trusted her and she talked to me on a soul level, the importance of which I could not deny.

Lucy was actually the first person I turned to for solace and guidance. Until then my inner struggle had been a solitary one. I knew her big laugh and deep, penetrating eyes would comfort me at a time when I was feeling fragile, frightened, confused and very vulnerable.

Late one night, sitting on her dock on the Indian River after a long drive from home, I revealed my plight to her. She listened attentively and compassionately while I talked about all the things that were happening to me. And then she read me the riot act. She confronted me, frankly but kindly, about how I had neglected my body and my health by working too hard, playing too hard, partaking of too many substances and placing myself under constant stress. Her assessment was difficult to hear, but on the deeper levels I welcomed it as the truth. In her own life, she told me, she planned pockets of time for health and relaxation and suggested, among other things, that I do the same.

Perhaps an even greater gift to me was to invite me into her healing room for a healing session so powerful that I remember it in detail many years later. The most amazing part of the session involved images of kind-hearted beings from another planet who had medical tools far exceeding those of earth and had come to this place to heal me. Lucy in weaving her meditation visualized that they examined me and then used their instruments to extract from my body the toxins and viruses that had incapacitated me. I can still vividly picture her description of the viruses leaving my body. She told me they lined up like stick men, and then marched single-file to their space vehicle, leaving the planet with a kindly good-bye.

While this sounded strange at the time, I couldn't deny the experience of an extraordinary healing. "What a creative process," I thought to myself. I sensed that Lucy had received higher guidance for her work with me, and I felt deeply blessed by this experience. This was the first time I had recognized blessings in the several months since my illness. I had been so submerged in the darkness of my illness that I couldn't see any light.

Before I left, Lucy recommended an alternative health facility, the famous Hippocrates Institute, then in Boston, as the place to begin my healing. Since I had little energy available to me, she suggested that I attempt to gain some control over my physical body as my highest priority. She felt that if I could master this difficult raw foods program, I might begin the long walk back to health.

I was reluctant to embark upon anything alternative. It was 1985 and, although my father had been gone for thirteen years, I continued to use his value system as the foundation for my guidance.

Dad was a brilliant tax lawyer, a lawyer's lawyer, who was considered the outstanding tax specialist in town and one of the finest in the Southeast. There was nothing in his background that touched upon anything off the beaten path. My younger brother, Neal, and I were taught the traditional ways of preparing for our futures as adult men: planning each step, building our resumes, being honest, playing fairly, competing vigorously and not taking advantage of others.

Sometimes when I recollect these values I recall the Boy Scout motto we recited so many times--"trustworthy, loyal, helpful, friendly, courteous, kind, obedient, cheerful, thrifty, brave, clean and reverent." There was not much in the way of risk-taking, adventure or creativity in these models, and neither Dad nor the Boy Scout motto suggested any benefit to experimenting "outside the box." In fact, a cornerstone of our upbringing was that we not stand out or deviate from the norm in any way.

I laugh when I remember the story of Dad's only traffic ticket. He received it while driving with my mother on a golf vacation to the North Carolina mountains. When a highway patrolman stopped Dad on the interstate, my mother vigorously protested that they were not speeding and had run no red light. The officer told them, instead, that unfortunately he had clocked Dad as traveling below the minimum speed limit and ticketed him for driving too slowly.

Dad was impeccably honest which, at times, he carried to an extreme. If his quarter bounced out of the tollbooth, he would stop the car, get out in the middle of traffic, and retrieve the change to make certain the toll collectors were not short-changed.

As a young man I believed that Dad's brilliance was unequaled. This brilliance and his measured speech gave him a presence that was powerful, albeit never flamboyant. When he spoke, everyone listened. I recall one dinner party where there was endless social chattering that typically annoyed me. Dad had settled unassumingly into his usual chair, mostly listening, with his trademark scotch and soda in his right hand, when someone posed a question to the room. He suddenly cleared his throat as if about to speak, and the room came to a jolting silence. All necks simultaneously craned toward him to see what he was about to say. He spoke with much authority, picking and choosing his words as carefully as if he were treading through a minefield.

Dad had been valedictorian of his high school, second in his class at Yale, and an editor of the *Harvard Law Review*. He had taught himself accounting at night while practicing law with a prestigious New York law firm. When he returned home to Florida, he managed to score first in the state on the bar and the CPA exams, and his professional career continued with the same excellence. While I had the deepest love and respect for him, you might imagine that he was a hard act to follow.

In 1985, when I was considering enrolling in an alternative health program as a way to regain my strength, I wondered what my father would have done in the same circumstance. Our role models may die, but their teachings and examples often remain with us throughout our lives. In this case, because of Dad's conservative lifestyle, I found it difficult to give myself paternal permission to head out into the unknown.

But in reality, at that point I seemed to have no other choice. Mainstream health modalities offered no immediate help or promise, and I desperately wanted to return to work as soon as I could. Among other things, if I went back to the office within the next few months I would be entitled to a low-risk economic interest in a downtown office building my partnership was buying, which could be very profitable for me over time. Even with this additional incentive, no small matter in those days, I couldn't muster the energy to return to work.

I departed for Boston and the Hippocrates Institute, as Lucy had recommended, as soon as it would have me and I was capable of getting myself onto an airplane.

Unbuttoned / Ken Fink

Chapter Three

PATIENT, HEAL THYSELF

"The doctor of the future will no longer treat the human frame
with drugs, but rather will cure and prevent disease with nutrition."
THOMAS EDISON

Unbuttoned / Ken Fink

efore my illness I had never heard of alternative medicine. My family typically went to the family doctor, who treated us for our complaints; on rare occasions, he sent us to a specialist. This usually was the extent of any medical search.

After I became ill, I began to hear of people with either severe and persistent conditions, or maladies that defied any existing medical classifications. When they couldn't find the help they needed from traditional medicine, they began to look into nontraditional approaches and systems. Soon, I found there was a wealth of help and healing available.

I now understand that something quite amazing happens when one commits wholeheartedly to a particular course of action. Avenues to that goal are revealed of which one had no awareness before making the commitment. This became strikingly apparent to me after I became responsible and proactive for my own return to health.

When I traveled to the Hippocrates Institute, I had no idea what I was getting myself into. The program was difficult, to say the least. I half-jokingly called it "a boot camp with sprouts." It focused primarily on my dietary intake. The only foods I ingested during my several weeks there were raw vegetables, many of them sprouted, and green drinks made from chlorophyll products such as kale, spinach and turnips. I felt this was all way over my head. Before the program, I had never heard the word "tofu," no less seen it – in a market or on a menu. I was a meat and potatoes man: barbecued spareribs, preferably with extra hot sauce, and maybe a gin and tonic or two to wash it down. Nothing looked the least bit familiar in the Hippocrates kitchen, and it took awhile to adjust to the unfamiliar garden smell from fresh green vegetables permeating the air.

During the course of the program, we were taught how to grow our own sprouts from seeds, which we did by planting them in dirt on cafeteria trays. We then cut our own sprouts and liquefied them with vegetables in one of the large juicers lined up in the vast Hippocrates kitchen. The purpose of the education was to prepare us to maintain the program once we returned home. The green drinks were, in fact, powerful energy builders and immune system enhancers.

Not surprisingly, I felt totally out of place in this alien environment, a neophyte organic farmer pretending not to be a buttoned-up lawyer. Inspired by Popeye, the only model I had for this kind of regimen – you'll recall that he ate his spinach for strength and so he could show off bulging muscles to Olive Oyl – I dutifully downed my veggie drink.

The feelings of deprivation – three meals a day of vegetables only for a committed carnivore – showed up in a recurrent dream I labeled "My Cheeseburger Dream." In it, I'm driving south on the Florida Turnpike and, suddenly famished, stop to get something to eat at a gas station. The only food offered is a cheeseburger. I loved cheeseburgers, particularly with mustard, pickles, and onions, the type Jimmy Buffet sings about. But downing a cheeseburger would be a horrific violation of my new diet. I summon all of my will power and turn my back on the beef, courageously resuming my trip with my bag of greens at my side.

When I awoke the next morning, I felt momentarily proud that my willpower had out-wrestled temptation, albeit only in a dream.

However, a full conversion was not yet a fait accompli; I would be revisited almost nightly with acts of seduction by well-pickled burgers.

The extent of my illness was undeniable. Many people in the program had cancer and other life-threatening illnesses, and their dedication and discipline helped me tough it out. There would be no chocolate mint on my pillow or glass of red wine before I turned in for the evening, and I gradually accepted the reordering of my eating priorities.

The program stressed the intake, by whatever orifice, of the greatest amount of wheatgrass juice possible. Wheatgrass is a sprouted sweet grass made famous by Ann Wigmore, the founder of the Hippocrates Institute. She believed that wheatgrass is one of the most, healing substances on earth because of its concentrated levels of chlorophyll. Its preparation requires juicing in a special juicer; the one at Hippocrates weighed more than a hundred pounds. Growing and juicing wheatgrass is a cumbersome ordeal, but taking it into the body is just as big a challenge. If taken through the mouth, the drink is consumed in small quantities, an ounce or two at a time, and is swallowed in one gulp, much like a tequila shooter without the lime or salt. People actually called it a shot of wheatgrass. It's very sweet. It also tended to make some visitors, including myself, nauseated.

The other method of getting wheatgrass into the system is by wheatgrass enemas. There's the low enema, a bulb syringe with a one-inch insertion piece similar to the kind used to aspirate a baby. It shoots the wheatgrass into your bottom and is held for as long as possible, so that it permeates the colon. For those who wanted to go the whole nine yards, there was the high enema, the Cadillac of wheatgrass ingestion. Here a large enema bag full of wheatgrass is inserted through a tube a couple of feet long. We were told this allows the wheatgrass to permeate and cleanse the liver, the master cleanser of the immune system. The Hippocrates Institute believed that restoring the liver to good health is a way to help heal all diseases.

Before I got to the Hippocrates Institute, I had no idea where my liver was. When I discovered it for the first time, I marked the corresponding location on my skin with a pencil so I wouldn't forget; it was a major key to my healing process. Traditional medicine recognizes that a high consumption of alcohol and prescription drugs are bad for the liver, but it attends to the liver only when diseased, and even then not very well. In alternative medicine, there are many proactive methods used for cleansing the liver, including wheatgrass and coffee enemas. Among the other systems that I learned about were liquid fasts, nutritional supplements, herbs such as milk thistle—widely used in Europe—and acupuncture for the liver meridians.

In the lives of most men, little attention was then given to health. Taking care of one's physical well-being was considered a sissy undertaking, especially among younger men. You just didn't do it if you were a strong, tough, macho man. If we didn't feel well, we were expected to tough it out. We bragged about our drinking contests and other, sometimes dangerous acts of bravado. Conversely, we were loath to talk about or attend to our injuries – physical, mental or emotional. It was only when someone we knew, especially a peer, died, or we personally became seriously ill, that our traditional male perspectives on health changed; it typically took something shocking to alter that perspective. Today many more men pay attention to their health, although it's still seen as a sign of weakness by some.

A few years earlier, a week before my marriage ended, my wife and I were one of two couples who drank $75 worth of tequila shooters—at a buck each! —, in a rural Florida town after a football game. Many years before that, in law school, I had the dubious distinction of tying for the championship of the St. Patrick's Day green beer drinking contest. The result: I lay in bed the entire next day, missing all of my classes and feeling like hell. But, even so, it seemed like a major accomplishment at the time.

Now it was essential that I learn to be good to myself. I was becoming committed to cherishing and supporting my good health. Over time I would experience many forces – from both the visible and invisible worlds – that would assist me in that commitment.

There were two minor downsides to my new focus on colon and liver cleansing. One was that I lost my taste for chopped liver, long a family favorite. The other was the realization that I had unmistakably entered middle age and it was here to stay. Would my definition of the crossover point – when one thought more about bowel movements than orgasms – be true for me, as well? Not a happy thought.

This was one of the lowest points in my life; I felt like giving up. That was very uncharacteristic of me. One night, I became lost walking the streets of Boston in a subfreezing rain. I felt sick and helpless, had no energy, and was frustrated that I still didn't have a credible diagnosis – did I have cancer or AIDS, or something equally foreboding? I didn't look forward to returning to the Hippocrates Institute's strange building with its unfamiliar steam heat, enema schedules and pungent smell of chlorophyll wafting down the halls. I passed an FAO Schwarz and wanted to purchase holiday gifts for my children, but couldn't muster the energy to walk through the revolving doors. With my life force so weak, everything seemed impossible. Only a month before this moment, I could jog ten miles; now, I couldn't even shop for gifts for my kids.

Toward the end of the three-week intensive, I began to regain some energy. I had been gray and ashen when I arrived, but now my energy— *chi* in Chinese medicine—was beginning to return. Before I left Boston, I had the good fortune to have a personal meeting with Ann Wigmore. Our interaction was a powerful encounter; its impact continues to today. Ann had come to the U.S. from her native Europe when she was seriously ill with cancer and other chronic diseases; I was told she looked terrible and her naturally red hair had turned totally white. She was so ill on her arrival that she had to be carried from the airplane on a stretcher. She developed the Hippocrates program using the methods she discovered in her own self-healing process. The use of wheatgrass emerged, in part, from observing how animals healed; she watched them simply sit in the sun and graze on grass. At the time I met her, she was totally recovered, her hair again a bright red to match her fiery personality. She was a bundle of energy who worked with the Hippocrates Institute during the day and wrote late into the night.

In the course of our meeting, I received a stern lecture from her, the second from a woman in the last few weeks. Although I was feeling somewhat better, the fact that I was sleeping more than four or five hours a night was a clue to her my body was toxic and it was essential for me to continue with the program once I returned home. As with many great healers, Ann directed her efforts to what she felt was needed most. With the arrival of AIDS in the mid-80s, she turned her attention primarily toward sufferers from that terrible disease.

I later heard that Ann died about ten years later while trying to extinguish a fire in the old row house where she lived. It was a great privilege to have met her. Like the other pioneers who helped me and devoted their lives to healing the very ill, she was a true visionary in alternative health and a deeply compassionate healer.

After I completed the program in Boston, my spirits returned.

Now I was faced with another challenge; I needed to continue the raw foods program at home. I had few skills in the kitchen, and maintaining the time-intensive regimen of sprouting and juicing was pretty daunting.

At that point, an angel named Faye appeared suddenly, answering my silent cry for help.

Faye was from New Zealand; I had met her at the Hippocrates Institute. There, she had given me several reflexology sessions. Reflexology is a system in which precise accupressure points on the foot are massaged in order to stimulate various organs of the body. I had experienced reflexology some years before and knew that it worked. I suffered from a prostate infection, and my massage therapist suggested that reflexology might help. When she pressed gently on a precise point on the outside of my heel corresponding to my prostate gland, I almost jumped off the table. But I was unquestionably better the next day.

When I eagerly took this new-found discovery to a urologist, my revelations were met with blank stares. I thought I was offering him a valuable tool in his medical practice, but it clearly was not welcome. In the late 80's and early 90's, practitioners of traditional medicine had little tolerance for the discoveries of alternative medicine. At best, they dismissed these practices as unproven; at worst, they regarded alternative medicine as quackery. Today, alternative practitioners in certain areas of the country are receiving more visits than traditional doctors. Some physicians have experienced personal illnesses or illnesses in their families which were successfully treated with alternative modalities and are now accepting these treatments as valid. Others have developed integrative medical practices, combining traditional and alternative therapies – the best of both worlds.

Faye had taken a liking to me and came to Florida to help me set up my program. I never could have done this on my own and was thankful that the Universe provided once again. In addition to working with my food, she counseled me on exercise. Although I had been active all of my life, I now had little energy for any activity. But she dragged me onto the beach outside my home and forced me to walk several times a day. The relationship might have turned into something romantic or sexual, but for once in my life I had no energy or desire for that. Faye's last wish before she returned to New Zealand was to visit nearby Disney World. This did not seem like much to ask, but it was quite a stretch for me with my "thimble" of energetic reserves. However, I was very grateful to her and wanted to honor her wish and so, as gently as possible, we had our Disney Day – abbreviated but full of heart.

During my stay at the Hippocrates Institute, I also had an eye-opening exchange with a woman from Boston. Heidi would wake up around 4:30 a.m. and meditate for a couple of hours before the day began, certainly before my day began. In my ignorance, I teased her about why she would lose two hours of sleep to sit in silence when she could have slept until the sun rose. She was good-natured about the kidding and didn't challenge or disagree with me. To her, there was nothing to prove. I did not understand what meditation was, nor did I know of its benefits, so she let me drone on in my ignorance.

We decided to share two evenings and treat each other to an adventure. My adventure consisted of an evening at Boston Garden to see the Boston Celtics and the great Larry Bird. Heidi was a good sport and seemed to genuinely enjoy the game. For her outing, she took me to an ashram, The Brookline Center devoted to the practice of Siddha Yoga as taught by Gurumay, a much revered Indian spiritual teacher with a large following that included such familiar cultural faces as John Denver. Heidi lived in Guramayi's main U.S. ashram, in South Fallsburg, New York. I wasn't excited about Heidi's choice for the evening, but wanted to honor her invitation.

When I arrived at the ashram, I was struck by its beauty. The bright colors and decorative pieces had a powerful effect on my senses. It was what I might imagine the Taj Mahal in miniature would look like. I had a negative preconception about ashrams and Indian practices and anticipated an unappealing, uncomfortable evening. Instead, when the chanting and meditation finished a few hours later, I found myself in a state of great calmness and peace. My judgments had been replaced by bliss!

This experience cracked open a door to Eastern spiritual practices through which I would jump through with both feet soon thereafter. I was clearly out of my element that evening, but my openness allowed seeds to be planted in my subconscious. Within the next year I would be spending huge chunks of time in a yoga ashram deepening my learning process.

I doubt that the Boston Celtics had a comparable effect on Heidi.

Unbuttoned / Ken Fink

Chapter Four

RECEIVING GUIDANCE

"The finest emotion of which we are capable is the mystic emotion.
Herein lies the germ of all art and all true science. Anyone to whom
this feeling is alien, who is no longer capable of wonderment and
lives in a state of fear, is a dead man..."
ALBERT EINSTEIN

Unbuttoned / Ken Fink

*I*n the life I was leaving behind I had felt a certainty about my goals and what I needed to do to reach them. There was a sense of safety and comfort in knowing where I was going. If I seemed to get lost, I had familiar guideposts, a kind of life compass, to steer me in the right direction.

On this new path I was walking, I felt lost, the hand of the compass now feverishly swirling in no fixed direction. I once used the analogy of walking through mud in the middle of a swamp. I couldn't see solid land in any direction; any forward movement was near-impossible. I had not yet learned to trust my instinct in deciding which directions to take.

If guidance for my life's problems and goals did not appear naturally, I would, as they say in modern jargon, become proactive. The guidance I had previously sought usually concerned issues of my material world. I sought advice mostly from professionals – doctors, lawyers, accountants, brokers and financial planners. At that time, I also frequently gave advice concerning worldly issues; seeking guidance went hand-in-hand with giving it. In my twenties and thirties, my colleagues and I would often swap information. I would advise a stockbroker friend on his corporate or legal questions, for example, and he in turn would advise me on my stock selections. Giving advice made me feel important and worthwhile, and receiving advice helped me to feel supported.

When I now reflect on some of the formal advice I gave through legal opinions, I question if they were of much value. These opinions were based upon certain assumptions offered in the context of my professional assessment. Each opinion was then made subject to a variety of conditions, caveats and qualifications. In addition, there might be weasel words or phrases such as "probably," "unless," or "in the preponderance of circumstances," words that allow attorneys myriad avenues of escape, or "outs". It often seemed that what we gave with one hand we took back with the other. We usually sought a balance between allowing a client to go forward with what he or she wanted to do, while at the same time protecting ourselves against the course of action going bad and the possibility of the client suing the law firm. There was always the threat, mostly implicit; that we could lose the future business of a client if we failed to give him what he wanted. This is not to say that we would give incorrect, inaccurate, or untruthful opinions, since we did not, but we tried to be accommodating.

As securities lawyers, the prospectus we prepared to describe an offering was intended to give potential investors guidance. But this document was so complex, voluminous and convoluted that it was almost impossible to figure out the salient points. The relevant issues might have been buried within a financial footnote or obscured hundreds of pages into the document.

As an investor, I never read a prospectus. It does not really inform, although millions of dollars might be spent in its preparation. Even if it's not really useful, the fact that a company would be required to describe its business and operations in a public document open to the scrutiny of many professional eyes has some prophylactic effect on its willingness to deviate from sound and honest activities. Companies tended to clean up their accounting practices, self-dealing or questionable business practices to a certain degree when detailed public disclosure was mandated.

Medical guidance tends to be similarly clouded. For example, a doctor might advise me to take a certain drug, but if I read the caveats on the drug inserts, even for drugs very commonly prescribed, I would be loath to take it. The physician may tell me the medication would be helpful and safe, but the insert would warn that the medication might give me a stroke, seizure, heart attack, paralysis, nausea, bad breath, or even rare forms of athlete's foot. Consequently, I have been advised to take it and not take it simultaneously.

When I first became ill, I began to look for direction from untraditional and alternative health and spiritual sources. I found this new information to be immediately useful, and I was grateful for it. In hindsight, it was not that what I had done previously had failed; its time had come and gone, at least for now, and I was ripe for different input.

One of the first people from whom I sought guidance was a spiritual teacher and clairvoyant from my hometown named Jill. I had been taking Jill's spiritual awareness class since my divorce, but had never had a reading with her. I now sought her help to identify my illness. I was still having severe fatigue and swollen glands and I feared I might have something life-threatening like cancer or AIDS.

Jill told me without hesitation that I didn't have either of these dreaded diseases and advised me to confirm with a physician that there was nothing fatally wrong with me. It was a huge challenge at that time for me to believe that I wasn't dying, but somehow Jill's lack of equivocation, qualification or hesitation impressed and reassured me. I had become an expert craftsman of equivocating legal opinions; conversely, her clarity and directness – which she quite willingly recorded on audiotape – had a ring of authenticity to it.

The day after I cleaned out the trunk of my car for the first time in five years, Jill gave me the reading. Her opening remarks connected right away: "I see you cleaning out your life both physically and internally." During another reading, prior to an appointment with my doctor to check my apparently racing heart, Jill said, "I see your heart racing. They (her spiritual guides) want me to tell you it is not a physical problem, it's anxiety." This saved me a doctor's fee, plus unneeded worry.

I found it fascinating that useful information could come from sources and methods other than mental analysis. An entirely new world had opened for me; after a long period of stagnation, my life began to feel expansive. Perhaps for the first time in this lifetime, my curiosity was now totally engaged on my own behalf. I came in contact with more and more people who were carrying out their lives upon the guidance of their personal meditations or prayers. Now, I was one of them; I began to receive readings more frequently. These new sources of information were not subject to traditional methods of proof; they seemed derived from a higher source and turned out to be quite trustworthy.

The following year, 1986, during a trip to Santa Fe, I stopped at the well-known spiritual Ark Bookstore, to inquire where I might get a psychic reading. Although I was not yet convinced of the validity of these services, I sensed I could find help through them in seeking new directions to my life. My entire existence and value system were under a microscope at this time, so I was willing to turn to these often strange sources for information, especially when the referrals came from new friends I had come to trust.

At the Ark, it was suggested that I call Chris Griscom, who had received recent publicity as Shirley McLaine's spiritual counselor. In turn, Chris suggested that I call a clairvoyant named Kali, named after the Hindu goddess. After I made an appointment to see Kali the next day, I received a Tarot reading. This is a centuries-old divination method that is interpreted through a deck of symbolic cards known as the Tarot. The reader told me I had chosen "the path of transformation," one of the most difficult. I could not grasp what she meant; in my naiveté, I thought that since I was used to easily succeeding at difficult things, it would be a piece of cake. Within the next couple of years, I came to learn the challenges would be more like wrestling a bear; almost everything I held to be important would be challenged or shattered. The next day, accompanied by a friend from California, I located Kali in an unmarked house about 20 miles from town. She lived there with many dogs, so it was a madhouse with all the barking. The circumstances were so bizarre that I couldn't help wondering how on earth I had been led here; I could not possibly have drawn up this game plan consciously.

Before I sat down, Kali stunned me by saying, "I see you just had a reading by the cards." She went on to say that the information given to me was correct, but the time frame was not accurate and the changes would occur more rapidly than I had been advised. She also talked at length about each of my three children and the effects of my divorce on them. She was able to describe each of their essences and even captured minor subtleties of their personalities. "How could she possibly know all this?" I asked myself, impressed with her information and accuracy.

I didn't yet fully believe in psychic ability and wondered how this mysterious woman in a shack 1,700 miles from home could provide wise counsel for me and my children. But the depth and truth of this encounter with Kali permanently changed my perspective. I also continued to seek clarification of my medical situation, and almost all of my travels included this as the primary objective. My medical diagnosis had remained quite vague, and I was still intent on getting a credible diagnosis and relief from my debilitating fatigue, almost unrelenting anxiety, terrible indigestion and painful, swollen glands. While this conflagration of symptoms was being labeled as chronic fatigue syndrome, traditional doctors told me that they couldn't put a name to what I had. Even if they could, there was nothing they could do for me on a physical level.

I began to question my old skepticism about pursuing so-called "alternative" medicine. I realized that it was a misnomer to include all alternative medical systems under the New Age banner, since many of these systems had been used very effectively for thousands of years. In comparison, Western allopathic medicine was only a few hundred years old. While in the 19th century doctors began using such useful methods as tasting the urine of their patients to diagnose diabetes, they were also still applying leeches to patients to cure other diseases. This realization helped me begin to open to health and healing systems I had, until then, regarded as somewhat hokey.

Around this time, I met Linda, a physical therapist whose diagnosis and treatment methods went far beyond the usual parameters of physical therapy. A good friend had highly recommended her, so I decided to contact her for input toward a diagnosis and help with treatment options. Until she and I actually connected, I was skeptical I could be helped by someone known more for her intuitive talent than vigorous medical training. But I found Linda to be extraordinarily gifted and possessed with a heartfelt, genuine intent to help me heal.

When Linda stood next to me and put her hands on me, she was able to read much of my past and present medical history. She began by accurately reporting I had mononucleosis when I was 18. Indeed, that first semester of my freshman year of college was a rough time; I was miserably sick for several months. Her uncanny perception quickly gained my attention. I knew Linda was tuned to the right frequency. She then intuitively scanned each organ and system in my body, reported the extent of functionality by percentage, and then compared that with the average functioning at my age. She also told me to which diseases I would be most susceptible in the future. Of greatest value to me were her practical, useful recommendations for strengthening those areas that were weak or functioning poorly.

After completing the body scan, Linda told me I had three active viruses in my system and these were the cause of my problem. I returned with this information to my medical doctor, Dr. Jesse Stoff, who is a wonderful human being, national expert in immunology and viral illnesses, and author. Some time earlier and as a part of his program on chronic fatigue, Dr. Stoff had taken ten vials of my blood for testing. He was quite knowledgeable and used several modalities in his practice of integrative medicine to help me deal with the physical components of my illness. Dr. Stoff had reported only two of the three viruses to me. At my request, he thumbed through his records and told me that Linda was indeed correct. I did have three viruses, but he had mentioned only two since the third virus was not particularly germane.

I was further captivated by people who could offer me guidance from nonphysical and often unverifiable sources. Over time, it became clear to me that we all have an ability to receive information that comes from somewhere beyond our conscious knowing, whether or not we're willing to acknowledge it or its non-mental source. An important factor in accessing these inherent abilities seems to be releasing any fears we might hold about them. I'm not saying we're all able to be medical clairvoyants, but we are certainly able to receive and pass along information beyond what we consciously think we know.

I notice that the choice of words I use to suggest we all have innate knowing or extraordinary abilities tends to either raise curiosity or invoke fear—depending on whether I choose words with greater or lesser cultural acceptability and with whom I'm speaking. If I talk about "trusting your gut instinct," or "following your intuition," almost everyone knows from direct experience what I mean. But if I talk about "clairvoyant" information, or "healers," I notice that the listeners often glaze over and shut down. I've learned that if I want people I know to understand my experiences, and perhaps tap into them for guidance themselves, it serves both of us to use culturally mainstream language. This seems to bypass the fear phenomenon and help people be receptive to the help that's been so useful to me.

I could try to justify the reality of what I've experienced, but have found that most people don't change their minds about unproven or controversial phenomena because of another's reality. If change happens, it usually comes from their personal experience. I observed that a Los Angeles jury could not be convinced that Rodney King had been beaten, even though they watched videotapes that were clear and complete. It took a riot in the streets before people were finally able to accept what they had seen.

And so, I learned that guidance from nonverifiable sources and ancient traditions became useful to me. For this time period this new form of guidance substituted for guidance from verifiable and mainstream sources that I had relied on all of my life. I just needed to follow my instincts whatever the source of the information, which is an element of personal responsibility, nor surrendering my power to those who offered advice. Thus, when advice was given to me, whether from a verifiable or a mystical source, I learned to assess it through my personal sensing patterns, to see whether or not it fit. At times, I had been given some bad advice by well-respected authorities both personally and professionally, so now whether advice was sourced from mainstream or alternative sources became less important than whether it felt right to me.

Unbuttoned / Ken Fink

Chapter Five

A LAWYER MEETS A YOGI

"'Come in,' she said, 'I'll give you shelter from the storm.'"
BOB DYLAN

Unbuttoned / Ken Fink

ix months after my Hippocrates experience, my birthday was approaching and I had no plans. I was bored and looking for something new. Lucy suggested I attend a weekend workshop given by a man named Yogi Amrit Desai. He was in Florida to offer his annual weekend retreat.

I had never met anyone with the title "Yogi" and had virtually no idea of what that meant. I learned that Yogi Desai, affectionately known as Gurudev, or "beloved teacher," was the founder of the Kripalu Yoga Center in western Massachusetts, a large and respected retreat, health and spiritual center. I did not give much thought to the weekend and simply decided, with little advance research and few preconceived notions, to open to a new experience.

I quickly found I brought with me far more mental baggage than I might have thought. While I participated in the workshop, I did so tentatively; I did not want to become enamored with Indian yogis. I had judgments, born of ignorance, I realized only later, about everything from the use of incense and *pronaming*, or bowing reverently, to Gurudev's robes. I automatically judged what seemed familiar as good and what seemed unfamiliar as bad. I also felt I had wandered far enough from the mainstream, and the last thing I needed was to get involved with yet another thing that seemed weird. The notion of Ken Fink sitting and listening to the Guru would have been like the Woody Allen movie, *Hannah and Her Sisters*, in which Woody – the perennial neurotic – looks longingly over a fence at a group of Hare Krishnas and then takes communion on Christmas Eve at a Catholic church in spite of his Jewish upbringing. I absolutely did not want to become a fish dancing with butterflies.

But as strange as the experience with Gurudev seemed on one level, I undeniably felt a deep sense of peace in that environment. The words of the yogi were profound, deep and simple. I experienced a visceral knowing that I was in the presence of truth, at least that which was true for me. It had taken me some time to stop questioning the rightness of an action for myself when it felt so right inside. The simple directive of the writer Joseph Campbell, to "follow your bliss," was becoming profound guidance for me.

Amrit Desai did not want anything from me; that appealed to me. He did not want to convert me or have me join or contribute to anything. Also, he did not confine his teachings to lightness, joy and laughter, although he embodied these qualities himself and seemed to be having a hell of a good time. This was one happy, healthy guru. People came forward, one at a time, to talk with him about life problems with which they were dealing. It usually had to do with health, money, sex, relationships, time management or grudges, the kinds of issues we all meet at one time or another. I found his responses startlingly simple and wise and also broad enough to speak to others with similar concerns.

Intrigued, I decided to come forth to speak with him. My question was one I had been wondering about for a while: how could I avoid the same thoughts or thought processes repeating themselves over and over? I told him that this made me feel like a hamster running inside a maze from which I couldn't escape. He stopped me mid-question and with humor said, "It sounds like you're tired of listening to your own tapes." Then, with a huge smile, he pointed to a nearby table displaying his audio cassettes and said, "Why don't you try listening to mine?"

I purchased a couple of the tapes; over the next several weeks, I found myself playing them over and over. Their common sense wisdom was exciting to me. Among my favorites were "Breaking Free and Finding Peace", the kind of themes I was just discovering that I was eager to master. Of course, I would alternate his tapes with Bob Seger's *Night Moves* or Fleetwood Mac's *Rumours*; the last thing I wanted was to become one-dimensional! Over the course of my many years of healing I often replayed these tapes that I found to contain pearls of universal truths, especially if I was locked in negative thinking or focused on insignificant life details. Listening to them could often break the logjam and set my mind at ease.

It would be several months before I ventured from Florida to the Kripalu Yoga Center in Lenox, Massachusetts. It was now six months since my illness began. I was drawn to attend a fasting program I saw advertised in a national magazine. I had heard that fasting cleanses the system and could give a natural high, and I missed my artificially induced highs of days gone by. It also presented me with a challenge, like climbing a mountain in the world of experimentation with food, and I felt it might help toward restoring my health.

The week I spent on vegetable juices was one of the most powerful experiences of my life. Much to my surprise, there was little physical hunger. Without food to numb me out, however, the issues surrounding my emotional hunger had space to surface. This was the perfect place to confront those inner demons, since there were skilled facilitators available with whom I could process my experiences.

By the second day of the fast, I began to feel badly. My body was detoxifying by throwing off toxins into the blood stream. I felt lethargic and achy, which I had been told to expect. But by the third day the lethargy faded and my energy returned. I was on a natural high, which increased each day until the end of the week. My eyes grew clear and my thought processes became focused and crisp. Some days it actually felt good to be alive, which I hadn't experienced in many months. At the end of the fast, most participants did not want to stop fasting, since they felt so good. But, together with the others in my group, we met that most challenging piece of the process by breaking the fast gradually and consciously.

Several years later, my oldest child, Julie, joined me at Kripalu for a week-long juice fast. She was about to enroll as an undergraduate at Brandeis University and was preparing to try out for the cross-country team. During the fast, she had the best week of training in her life and set personal records for weekly mileage up and down the Berkshire Mountains. I admired her for the courage to try something so unfamiliar in order to share the experience with her father. I consider it an honor when someone close is willing to explore my environment with me, and I try to reciprocate. It is always a challenge to a relationship when one party is in a process of change; unless the other is willing to explore the new territory, the relationship can grow distant as one of the two now lives, at least part-time, in a different reality.

While at Kripalu. I took long walks in the Berkshires and enjoyed a presence with my surroundings that had been foreign to me not so long ago. I noticed the birds, flowers and the shapes of the trees as I walked nearby historic roads past Tanglewood, the summer home of the Boston Symphony Orchestra, and down Hawthorne Road, where Nathaniel Hawthorne wrote *The House of the Seven Gables*. I also roamed the beautiful 300 acres of the Kripalu land once owned by Andrew Carnegie.

I also began to be aware of this man Gurudev, who was responsible for this healing place with which I was so taken. I saw that he was always willing to experiment with new concepts that related to health, consciousness and spirituality, and I had great respect for this quality. He brought to his community nationally prominent teachers from diverse cultures, trainings and belief systems, including a variety of approaches to the practice of yoga other than his. He always seemed eager to learn and participate, and seemed to have no fear of the competition taking away some of his participants. When spiritual paths or teachers say "only my way," I run the other way. That rigidity, I believe, comes from being underdeveloped in certain respects, with the attendant fear that their weakness or the weaknesses of their teachings will be exposed.

I eagerly returned to the Kripalu Center many times during the next six or seven years. It became my home-way-from-home. I came to know the nearby towns and many of the people who lived in and around Kripalu. I also became familiar with the practices of the yogic community. I learned that bowing to the guru—which was not required and certainly not practiced by everybody—was not a gesture of deference. Rather, to hold the head below the heart was a sign of humility and humbleness. Guru, literally translated, means "from darkness into light", or to remove the blinders.

Conscious living and simplicity were cornerstones of Kripalu. For instance, the ingredients of all food offered were labeled in full detail. I liked this; otherwise, I wouldn't know what I was eating, which was important to me. People made every effort to live consciously. This was in sharp contrast to my former tear-'em-up pace, at which there was almost no time to think about where I was going because I was so preoccupied with getting there.

The people who worked at Kripalu – kitchen personnel, grounds people, housekeepers – gathered by groups each morning to process or discuss with their supervisors what they were feeling about their work, which they called *seva* or selfless service. This self-reflection was an essential cornerstone of conscious living at the center. Over time I witnessed many touching encounters in these gatherings, including the honoring of one department for another and with that the acknowledgment of their gracious interdependence. On Mother's and Father's Days residents posted photos of their mothers or fathers on the hallway walls, along with stories and poems expressing appreciation for their parents.

I found myself often moved to tears by these acts, reflecting an open-heartedness new and unfamiliar to me. On many occasions, I felt my heart open in this atmosphere that so deeply valued awareness, consciousness, compassion and service.

My personal health was the usual purpose for my visits, and my definition of health expanded greatly from my experiences at Kripalu. It was not only about what I ate, or how many classes I took, but about what I did with my thoughts and with the art of loving and forgiving. In the West, we may be willing to discipline ourselves around money, diet, house maintenance, appearance and personal grooming, but are unwilling to address our thoughts when they run amuck. I learned that in Eastern philosophy the mind is often discussed separately from the person, as if it were a distinct entity.

I came to see that my mind could be my friend or my foe. The Kripalu programs placed much emphasis on focusing my thoughts so that they were positive and affirming and also upon the use of meditation to quiet the mind. The emphasis in my formative years had been on intellectual knowledge and expression. This concept that my mind could undermine me if I failed to meet it properly was new to me and probably far more powerful than most of the values proffered through my years of school learning.

Since I had always been on the run, I was dumfounded at how difficult it was to sit quietly with no or few thoughts. Initially I considered myself to be one of the world's most agitated meditators. My mind raced and my body wiggled. When I was a young boy, I was reprimanded constantly for wiggling too much; now I had to deal with my restlessness again. In my orthodontist's chair I had been so impatient that when he left the room, I crawled out of the chair and began to experiment with its positions. Blood-curdling screams soon followed when the chair came crashing down on my head and I was pinned to the floor with my legs flailing in all directions. I was now ready to put this chronic restlessness behind me. But, with meditation, I was going one step further – actually attempting to enjoy being still and quiet and to immerse in that stillness.

The daily routine at Kripalu started around 5:30 a.m. with meditation, yoga and breathing practices, followed by a healthy breakfast. At 5:15 a.m., with a blanket around my shoulders among a hundred others silently walking beside me to similarly begin their day, I felt awake and alive in an entirely new way. I was also comforted by the silent presence of others and our common yearning for wholeness, even though there were often few words between us. This silent, shared togetherness gave me a deep feeling of peace, the peace of coming home to myself.

One aspect of Kripalu that fascinated me was that celibacy was required for unmarried permanent residents. Consequently, men and women were often physically separated as part of the practice of *bramacharya*, moderation in all things. Celibacy among young adults was probably the most difficult barrier for the residents. As a guest, I was not subject to those rules, but those who were had a constant struggle with it. I would encounter women in whom I felt that steam was literally emanating from their sexual organs.

Those who practiced celibacy worked at transforming sexual energy into a higher spiritual energy. In theory, it was not a practice of denial. I was aware that one contemporary Indian teacher encouraged open and free sexuality as a path to God among his large following; he taught that releasing, rather than transmuting or withholding sexual energy, could awaken higher consciousness. It was interesting that placing severe restrictions on sex *and* embracing a great freedom in sexual practices were both considered pathways to the Divine. This reflected an understanding that human sexual energy has higher as well as lower implications.

The food at Kripalu was delicious and it changed my conception of vegetarian meals, which, until then, made me feel like a grass-grazing cow. A local shopkeeper said to me that the famous New York restaurateur Vincent Sardi told him Kripalu had the best food he had ever eaten. Several times while I was there, Gurudev led us in conscious eating exercises. These were silent meals during which he led the diners through a process of chewing each bite of food two hundred times and each bite of soup one hundred times before swallowing. Sometimes, in my normal routine, I would literally ingest my food like a vacuum cleaner, so even ten chews was a great meditation and health practice for me.

One frequent visitor to Kripalu was Dr. Deepak Chopra, who the community always found delightful and interesting. He was then in the early stages of achieving his international fame as an author, speaker and world visionary. One of the great pioneers in the understanding of health and human consciousness, Dr. Chopra has been particularly instrumental in articulating the mind-body connection, emphasizing that the mind and the body are one. Every thought we have, he teaches, immediately impacts every cell of our body. Gurudev often spoke on this same theme, and I embraced it wholeheartedly. A poster I brought home reads, "You are the creator. Whatever you believe, that is what you create, and that is what you become."

There were many new levels of awareness I achieved at Kripalu. One was to meet men who were soft and loving and to discover that there was no disgrace in showing one's feelings. Flexibility in body and spirit were emphasized, and strength was measured by the ability to grow, learn, forgive and engage in selfless service – not by brute force. I also began to consider that my illness, now diagnosed by at least one doctor as chronic fatigue syndrome (CFS), carried with it a message – as do all illnesses. In biofeedback sessions with a staff doctor, I would see someone pulling on a horse's reins, calling out "whoa!" I understood that to be a communication telling me to slow down. Were all the bouts of pain, lethargy and problems of digestion my body's way of telling me to stop? Astrologically, my birth chart – often understood as the seed plan for one's life – had a heavy Aries focus, with my sun, moon, Mercury and Venus in that part of the heavens. This represents the presence of a lot of fire. Aries also are most likely to suffer burnout. It was becoming increasingly clear to me that, to slow down, I needed to learn to alter my basic make-up. Slowing down would also help me with the anxiety either causing or caused by the CFS.

I began to feel I had lived like the 60s' Jackie Gleason TV character, Reginald Van Gleason, when he was preparing martinis for a large party. Reginald tended bar behind a conveyor belt where, as the glasses moved down the belt, he would slowly, calmly and with great confidence place the ice, then the gin, then the vermouth and finally the olive into one martini glass after another. As the demand for drinks accelerated, the belt accelerated as well, until finally, with Reginald on overload, absolute chaos ruled and martinis were flying throughout the banquet room.

Part of the pressure of legal practice that had been the most psychologically difficult for me was the pressure around billable and collectible hours. In those days my hourly rate started at $125, and my monthly budget at 140 hours – a mere pittance at today's rates. Three months later the rate climbed to $150 and the budgeted hours rose to 160. Spreadsheets were handed out each month showing who had met and exceeded their budget. I hated having to conform to this pressure, but I also didn't want to fail to meet budget or look bad competitively. Like the pressure on Reginald Van Gleason, as soon as I met one level of expectation, the bar was raised. One day I noticed I was reluctant to go to the bathroom for fear I would fail to meet my budget. I started to evaluate life in terms of budgeted and billable hours. A good morning in the toilet with the Sunday newspaper might have cost $30 at yesterday's rates and $90 or more at today's rates! I have a lot of compassion for people in the work force who must meet budgets of one kind or another and deal with the oppressive application of these rules when times get economically tough.

I liked the idea that illness offered us messages to further our personal evolution. I preferred a purpose or message to my illness rather than the thought that I was arbitrarily taken out by an unidentified virus. It made sense to me that one could discern order in the Universe and meaning in the major events in our personal and collective lives. With this new understanding, my mind raced to order events that seemed chaotic to me and to find meaning in everything that was problematic. I soon realized that this was impossible, that there was also a grand mystery to it all. At times, it was far better to give up trying to understand and instead to just be in the midst of inexplicable occurrences – a challenge of a different kind for someone like me who had put such a high value on control.

With a history of "success" achieved by pushing through my problems, running the extra mile, bench pressing ten more pounds, or writing one more redraft, it was a revelation to me that these distortions of the masculine principle were working in reverse for me and inevitably were the source of failure. If I pushed too hard or too long, they would manifest as relapse. It was through aspects of the feminine principle – listening, compassion, touching, healing, nourishing – that my illness was being healed. I needed to create an identity around being rather than doing. Like most men, I had measured myself by my performance with such things as jobs, bank accounts, sports and sexual conquests. That had to change.

I drove an old 1985 black Delta 98 Oldsmobile with 150,000 miles up to New England. I did not have the strength to make the exhausting drive back to Florida and so decided to leave it near Kripalu, along with a trunk full of winter clothes, for use locally and to reduce expenses when I traveled north.

Kripalu became a spiritual, as well as a healing, home for me during the first part of my journey; I found myself as comfortable there as I had ever been, anywhere. But while Kripalu served as my place of refuge until Gurudev's forced resignation in the early 1990s, I felt no need to become a formal disciple. Today I regard Gurudev as one of the great teachers on my path. The effects of those many journeys to Massachusetts generated immediate and amazingly long-term ripples that touched and impacted every shore of my mind, body and being.

Unbuttoned / Ken Fink

Chapter Six

REACTIONS, PROJECTIONS, REJECTIONS

"Don't clap too much one day because you will boo too much the next, and whether you clap or boo has much more to do with you than with me."
YOGI AMRIT DESAI

Unbuttoned / Ken Fink

*W*hen people change, others often project their realities onto the one making the change. If they have longed for freedom from responsibility, they might project that their friend is searching for freedom. If they wish they could sexually experiment, they will conclude the other's changes are about free sex.

In a similar way, not all of my family, friends or acquaintances supported the changes I was making in my life. One-woman friend was afraid her husband might "catch a change in life direction" from me. She treated what I was doing as a disease, "Mad-Lawyer-Gone-Awry-Syndrome," against which her husband needed to be vaccinated. She believed he could be immunized against the "path less traveled" by keeping him away from my influence. I had left both my marriage and my profession, which were her two greatest fears about her husband. She lived in high style, for which she was dependent upon her husband; he was the source of both her financial well-being and her status in the community. If he attempted any change, she would have to do the work, herself, in those areas. Unfortunately, he obliged and stayed some distance from me. This distancing was painful to me because I had cherished his personal companionship; we could have shared some of the journey together to our mutual benefit.

Other people projected their positive fantasies onto me. Once, I was pulled aside at a cocktail party by an acquaintance, a money manager, who wanted to confess his most sacred secret. He leaned over my shoulder and covertly cupped his hands before whispering into my ear, his eyes roaming furtively around the room to assure that no one could hear us. His adulation was unmistakable; he told me I had become his hero. Because I didn't work six days a week, as he did, he believed I had beaten the system. He confessed it had always been his fantasy to take off a chunk of time and live as a mountain man in the Great Smoky Mountains of North Carolina. He dared not let this wonderful dream be known, for fear of losing his job, and had not even told his wife.

His revelation dampened my ears and sharpened my awareness of how imprisoned so many men feel within their lives. He exemplified the degree of fear we have about sharing what is real and significant to us, even with intimate friends. We often feel it's dangerous to move beyond superficial conversation and are wary of revealing our vulnerabilities, lest they make us seem less than the ways we want to appear. That certainly was the story of the first part of my adult life. In fact, the opposite is true: The more vulnerable we become, the more we seem to be loved. Once we let down the macho mask, it gives others permission to share their vulnerabilities, as well. Both parties find that each was not the only one who did not have everything in place emotionally or on the material plane.

Neither the positive nor negative projections of my family, friends and acquaintances really had anything to do with me. I had no intention of leading the woman's husband astray. Nor was I heroic in embarking on this transformational path, as my money manager friend believed. I initially made changes because I was sick and wanted to return to a healthy, functional and active life. For a long time, I didn't even have an idea I was involved in a transformational journey. In the midst of such battle or change, we often don't yet have a context or hindsight to recognize what is happening.

The most important part of what I was doing was the process itself; in order for me to continue to relate to family and friends, I needed the space and wanted their support, regardless of what my end point might be.

While having dinner with friends shortly after I took my leave of absence, one person I expected would support me spoke about another lawyer who recently left his practice. "He just couldn't hack it." Quite spontaneously, I choked on a mouthful of food and spit it all over the table; I was glad I did. I felt I was the unconscious target of the "couldn't hack it" comment, and I was enraged. After all, I had attended a nationally prominent law school and graduated in the top of my class. I had practiced with prestigious firms for fifteen years and progressed very well until I became too sick to continue. Later, I realized that I wouldn't have felt a need to defend myself so vigorously if a part of me didn't believe the assertion.

I didn't yet realize that the more I defended myself, the more susceptible I was to attack. To stop an attack is pretty simple: I simply stop defending myself. As for the comment about not hacking it, I realized the source of this comment was the critic's own projection of the fear of not being able to hack it in the work world. It was the other person's problem, not mine, a fact, which helped in many other seemingly humiliating situations I encountered over the years. The great American author Henry Miller summed up this tendency to project our inner demons onto others with his statement, "The study of crime begins with the knowledge of oneself. All that you despise, all that you loathe, all that you reject, all that you condemn and seek to convert by punishment springs from you."

Another particularly good friend also could not seem to tolerate my shift. When I met with him over lunch, I could feel judgments simmering beneath our chitchat. He would quickly find a way to elicit from me the admission I had no immediate intention to return to my law partnership. I couldn't have returned even if I wanted to, but my communicating that seemed to have little impact; he believed I was wasting my life until I did return. Some of the changes I was making would have helped round him out as a person, but ultimately he was unable to tolerate a life in the "gray zone;" our friendship dissolved. It saddened me; we had a lot of shared history and helped each other out on numerous occasions. But I had to let him go, like so many other people and things. I couldn't be with those whose actions were so well described by Albert Einstein: "Whoever undertakes to set himself up as a judge of truth and knowledge is shipwrecked by the laughter of the gods."

The friends who couldn't accept my new choices and ways of thinking disappeared and were quickly replaced by more broad-minded, less fearful people. As I struggled with my health and direction, I found these new friends prepared to embrace and accept me without judgment. As family members and other old friends faced their own traumas and dealt with inexplicable and difficult events over time, often having to search for answers and solutions outside the box, as I had done, they became more tolerant of the human dilemma – theirs, mine and others.

I found that I was befriended by a wide spectrum of people who were living original and self-directed lives. To them, my process of change was a normal part of life. In the life I was shedding, getting drunk or stoned, or taking three-week vacations instead of two, was as radical as people got. Now, I was often among people who were examining and redirecting their lives in major ways. I was pleased that many of my family and long-time friends stood firm and accepted and were interested in my journey. These were often people who, by circumstance or choice, had also lived outside convention on a short-term or permanent basis. To them, there was nothing unusual about my struggle.

Shortly after I became ill, I received what may have been a life-changing phone call from my good friend, Fred, who lived in California. First, some background: Fred and I had been close friends since our college days in Philadelphia. He had had a more sophisticated upbringing in New York, and I had come from a public school in Jacksonville. We met when I walked into the fraternity house for the first time, when he and his roommate came "jiving" down the stairs looking very cool. This was not my style. I was moderately conservative at the time, and thought to myself, "Fred and I will never have anything in common." Despite our initial superficial differences, I couldn't have been more wrong. Our relationship has stayed and deepened profoundly through the years, unlike so many male friendships based on collegiate camaraderie, which survive almost solely on reminiscences from the past.

Fred and I caught up with each other after a few years of being out of touch. I was in San Diego for a securities law conference and he had come to meet me there. I showed up in a white shirt, jacket and narrow tie, inconspicuous and "buttoned-up." In contrast, Fred had been impacted by life in California, where men had started to "feel." When he found me in the busy lobby of the upscale Hotel del Coronado, he threw his arms around me, burst into tears, and held his bearded cheek next to mine for some time. This public display of male affection was foreign to me, and I looked sheepishly around the lobby to see if anyone had noticed. Over time, I learned to be comfortable with and enjoy intimacy between men, but at this conference, Fred was way ahead of me.

Fred knew a lot about illness. A diabetic since age ten, he overcame many potential limitations. He was a star athlete in tennis, basketball and golf, and didn't let his illness stop him from living his dreams. He was also very active and important to the American Diabetes Association in its commitment to eliminate diabetes. Years later, at the fiftieth anniversary celebration of the American Diabetes Association, my son Ben and I joined Fred and his wife Marsha in Atlanta when he was one of the twenty or so people honored for their contributions during the association's first half-century. Other honorees included Ed Asner, Mary Tyler Moore, and several former presidents. Knowing the details of his struggles, I was particularly proud of this accomplishment.

When I was still in the early stages of illness, Fred asked me to describe the commitment I had made to my own health. His question caught me off-guard. I didn't know where he was going or how I was supposed to respond. Fred took the lead in the conversation and told me that he was one hundred percent committed to my return to health. When I asked him what he meant, his answers blew me away. He said that I could live with him in Los Angeles at any time. If I needed money, he would mortgage his house. If it was companionship I wanted, he would take a leave of absence from his job to join me in a place of healing.

I was deeply moved and taken aback by both the depth of his friendship and the strength of his commitment. I realized that my own commitment to my recovery, which I had considered to be pretty serious, was less than his commitment. This was a major turning point in my healing. It felt incredibly good to receive this kind of support, and I wanted to be worthy of his heartfelt offer. I could no longer avoid confronting in myself anything and everything that stood in the way of a total focus and commitment to getting well. Fred has been a continuous, substantial influence on my path, and he and Marsha continue to share many meaningful times with me.

During this time, my three children were still quite young, I felt sad about what they going through because of the complexities of my life. Their father was perceived by some among family and friends to have "fallen off the track." My seven-year-old son Ben, in particular, would repeat to me some of the things he was hearing – accusations that could not possibly have been dreamed up by a child. They clearly reflected the resentments of those who had grievances against me or lived in a fear-based reality.

These people also had difficulty understanding chronic fatigue syndrome. People with the disease look quite normal, which contributes to skeptical questioning if it's a legitimate illness and not simply malingering. I looked the same as I always had, but I was totally depleted and exhausted. At times, I could barely get up and go about my very simple daily routine. Also, the term "chronic fatigue" significantly understates the severity of the illness in a society where everybody is overworked. (Read the struggles of Laura Hillenbrand who wrote the best seller *Seabiscuit* while suffering from chronic fatigue syndrome.) I would hear all around me that others were tired, too. There were times when even Ben would tell me that he was too tired to do something he was supposed to do.

Few of my efforts toward healing or personal explorations into the great unknown produced anything meaningful in the larger scheme of things in terms of external rewards. There were no new cars, medals of commendation or bonus checks.

Both of my daughters, Julie and Allison, had clerked for my law firm one summer and so observed first-hand the qualities that had brought me to this conventional success. They were on their way to becoming lawyers and their exposure to my law practice that summer set the stage for their careers. I particularly felt badly for Ben, because he was five years old when I left his home, and I was not able to model for him the work ethic, studiousness and perseverance that had put me in the top of my class and brought me an early, impressive success. He had to rely on stories about me from the past; happily, the traditional behaviors I wasn't able to model for him were provided by others in his life.

There were also many blessings bestowed on us as a family by this uncanny illness. While my relationship ties had already been formed with my two daughters, without the illness I probably would not have had the exceptionally close relationship with Ben that developed through his college years. After my divorce, he spent most weekends with me and also many nights during the week. We established a pattern of speaking with each other several times a day when he wasn't with me. This frequency lasted until he found a steady girlfriend, but the depth of our relationship has remained intact over the years, for which I am profoundly grateful. He is a tremendous gift to my life.

I kept tabs on Ben in his formative years, not only when we were in the same town, but also when I was away. I would check on his schooling and his comings and goings. In turn, he would leave me messages about his arrivals and departures so I could be certain he was safely in the right place.

An unexpected gift of my illness was having time to bond and participate in my children's lives, which I would not have had other-wise. Ben said a couple of things about our relationship a few years ago that made me feel proud. He told his mother I had never acted in a way that put him down or diminished him. It was rewarding to hear this, and she was kind enough to share this with me. Later, when he was in his early twenties, he said, "Dad, isn't our relationship unusual? Do you know any father and son who have as close a relationship as we do?"

The most important and valuable qualities I modeled for my children, which they might not have been exposed to otherwise, had to do with choice. This included the permission and encouragement to make their own, unique, personal choices, to struggle for their freedom, and to choose paths of their own design. These teachings gave them the space to pursue lives based less on how things look or what people think, and more on following their own hearts.

When my daughters were older and came to me with questions, it usually involved them seeking approval for out-of-the-ordinary decisions. After hearing them out, I would often tell them that they knew their own answers. They had come to me instead of others because they knew my orientation would be to give them permission when they could not find it elsewhere. I came to see that, at subtle but profound levels, I was healing my entire family lineage. I was breaking from a tradition of black and white, of what's "utterly right" or "totally wrong". I felt I was paving the way for the generations to follow.

My illness and divorce naturally and inexorably changed my relationship with my children. I once heard it said that all a parent can give his children are roots and wings. Being in a separate household from them reduced my ability to provide a rooted sense of stability, but I have certainly presented each with a pair of golden wings.

I did not receive a lot of encouragement from some of those in my old, once formidable inner circle; it was painful to me. In their eyes, I had gone from being a shining star, or at least a slightly tarnished shining star, to a black sheep. On the other hand, I was not great at allowing the needs, sorrows and longings of my real self to be known. Because I was then unable to share my feelings, I hampered my own ability to receive nurturing from many I had known. This mirrors the traditional male pattern of suffering in silence and being stoic and brave whenever possible. Historically, the ultimate honor bestowed on men is for giving their lives for their country and not crying out in pain even when mortally wounded. I clearly bear a part of the responsibility in some of the breakdowns in my primary relationships.

The thought of going through life and not finding or manifesting my dharma haunted me, and I would panic when I considered that possibility. I would have the urge to rush out to find it, as if it were a lost wallet. This was as futile as trying to catch a fish with my bare hands. Instead, I needed to allow the answers to unfold and at the same time welcome those opportunities that spontaneously presented themselves to me. I believed that my trainings in the various alternative schools and centers of that time had something to do with discovering my life's purpose. Why else was I being cross-trained in disparate worlds? I sensed that the broad spectrum of my education – "from the boardroom to the ashram," I called it – gave me a unique perspective from which I could make a unique contribution. I had been respected and recognized for doing excellent work by my peers, yet I knew that legal work was no longer my life's calling. The illness had mandated this conclusion.

My father showed me that having the perspective available to him as a lawyer, a CPA and a tax expert gave him an advantage in all his business dealings. I thought that my cross training might give me an advantage, as well, in writing, teaching or otherwise communicating something of value to others. This thought inspired me, but occasionally I found myself stymied by so little appreciation from others. Clearly, I needed to move forward without the back pats to which I had become accustomed. I also needed to free myself from the effects of friends and colleagues constantly questioning what I was doing, which periodically took the wind out of my sails. I learned over time to be circumspect about what and with whom I shared about my journey. I learned to keep my mouth shut when I sensed what I had to say might trigger fear—sometimes expressed as attack, sometimes as aggressive questioning. This was difficult because of my passion for learning something and implementing it.

In time, I took acknowledgment of myself back into my own hands and patted myself on the back as often as possible. In the end, it was good for me, as are all such challenges.

Unbuttoned / Ken Fink

Chapter Seven

FROM HEROES TO HEROINES

"The feminine way is more cooperative than competitive; it
involves trust in intuition and thinking that is holistic,
multivariant and multidimensional. Most importantly,
'knowing' tends to be a relational thing, an ongoing process
between an individual and other persons, nature, a 'higher self,'
instead of a process of intellectual abstraction."

WILLIS HARMAN

Unbuttoned / Ken Fink

I n 1987, I was divorced. After a two-year leave of absence, I resigned my law partnership, certain that I would never again actively practice law. Two years earlier, I had sat at my desk the evening before I left, staring out from my 20th floor window at the lights of the empty business district below, and knew there was nothing more for me to do in this arena. Although I had planned on returning as soon as possible, when I closed the book in which I logged billable hours, my legal practice and that part of my life seemed surprisingly complete. Now, I no longer considered my new life and its strange adventures an unnecessary and uncalled for detour. It had become what my life was really about.

Until I embarked on my path of healing and spiritual realization, most of my heroes were men. I was raised in a household with strong patriarchal values. My father had three brothers and no sisters, as well as two sons and no daughters. The emphasis at home was always on our achievements. Would we become an Eagle Scout or the ace pitcher of our baseball team? How many ribbons could we win? Would they be blue first-place ribbons or red second-place ribbons? We were constantly building resumes for our later initiation into the world.

My heroes consisted of, first and foremost, my father. From there, the list included: Muhammad Ali, who I loved for his rebelliousness and willingness to tell the truth; Hardy Dillard, dean of the University of Virginia School of Law, who was my first-year contracts teacher; and my Rabbi, Sidney Lefkowitz. Three of these men were highly respected in traditional circles. At that time, Ali was an anti-hero who spoke to the restless and the radical. Rabbi Sidney Lefkowitz was right out of theological seminary when he was sent to the German front as an army chaplain. He was in his early 20s when, in a historically unforgettable moment, a photographer captured Chaplain Lefkowitz delivering the first religious service – he and his men still in trenches – after the allies invaded Germany. The service took place at the site of a concentration camp that had just been liberated. It was broadcast by radio around the world, and I can only guess at the extraordinary power of that moment, especially for Jews. When I attended his funeral in the 90's, I was deeply moved by objects at the altar from his military days, including the Bible he had held the day he spoke at the just-liberated extermination camp.

Rabbi Lefkowitz was philosophical and a scholar of the first order. I was consistently impressed by the breadth and depth of his understanding. He was my teacher in religious school and often drove my brother and me to Sunday school class and lunch afterwards. I sat in the front row and listened attentively to everything he said. He taught comparative religion at the local university for many years, and I especially liked that he was promoting peace and understanding between religions. He, like my father, used words carefully and precisely. I found him to be profound (although some of his young students might have wished him more exciting). Not surprisingly, he was highly regarded in the community.

Dean Hardy Dillard had the presence of a great southern orator. When I watched him in class, it reminded me of what I had read about the great Webster-Calhoun debates. His presence was spellbinding. He was a large man who would come to class looking distinguished in his three-piece gray suit and maroon ascot. When he spoke, he would pace the room from one side to the other and, with a deep southern drawl, wax eloquent with profundities about the greatness of the law. His lectures were replete with folklore and history, especially of the South, and were often interspersed with stories of the history of the University, which he spoke of as "Mr. Jefferson's school," referring to founder Thomas Jefferson. I loved the folksy examples he used to convey the essence of contract law. One I recall went like this: "Suppose you ran into Tim the Beggar sitting in front of the campus store and you said, 'Tim, I will give you a dollar if you shine my shoes,' and suppose Tim replied, 'I will shine your shoes for a dollar if I feel like it.' Do we have a contract, class?" I would look forward to those moments when he would throw off his jacket in the midst of making a point, like a workman suddenly rolling up his sleeves. Those dramatic flashes pointed us to the crux of whatever he was lecturing about.

We students would debate among ourselves whether or not there was a trace of bourbon on his lips, but we knew he held himself to the highest standard of excellence in class. He went on to further an already distinguished career by serving as the United States representative to the International Court of Justice. Hardy Dillard embodied to me all of what a lawyer should be: bright, practical, eloquent and always considerate of the historical and philosophical context of the questions at hand.

I find it interesting that three of my role models – my father, Dillard and Lefkowitz – were scholars who studied vigorously, were precise and erudite and whose communication styles were riveting. Two were reserved, refined and unassuming; Dillard was refined but never reserved. Ali, on the other hand, represented very different qualities. He was physical, unrestrained, carnal and outlandishly vocal. He was raw and rebellious and never seemed concerned what others thought of him. It seemed to me that something new and original was continuously showing up in him. I didn't know it at the time, but these were characteristics of my shadow side, those parts of me not yet known, embraced, expressed. The way in which I was enamored with Ali, I see now, pointed to the likelihood that he had something I wanted. Unlike my other heroes, he had broken from tradition and shattered the mold of the quiet, unassuming athlete. I, too, needed to break from the mold in which I had been cast.

At this time I did not have women heroes. My upbringing gave little emphasis to emotional well-being, feelings, intimacy, nurturing or the quality of receptivity. Not that these were disparaged; they just weren't given priority. Part of this imbalance in favor of masculine qualities seemed to come from my lineage and part was a product of the times. My mother served the family in the traditional role of mother and wife. Her focus was on bringing up her children, preparing meals and tending the house. She also provided the emotional foundation for the household, which I experienced as love and empathy, and she modeled friendship and other relationships through her very active social life. She and my father had been childhood sweethearts; her main function in life, as she viewed it, was to support Dad in his profession. She took care of everything that didn't absolutely require his attention so he could concentrate on his work.

Since my illness, the masculine approach on which I had been raised, which once worked so well in solving problems, now often proved to be counterproductive. I interpreted this, in part, as the Universe showing I needed to explore other ways to be effective. These, I would learn, included attributes of the feminine principle – a universal aspect quite foreign to me at the time. Once outside the traditional work environment, my daily interactions were now usually with women. I sometimes took a morning aerobics class I jokingly called the "housewives class." One day, at the end of the class, I had an epiphany: not only was I the only man in the class, but also it had taken me fifty minutes to notice.

I had been around a lot of what I call "the unhealed feminine" throughout my life, as have we all. These include such behaviors as whining, manipulation, seduction and betrayal. While they are not unique to women – both sexes have healthy and distorted masculine and feminine aspects –they more commonly find expression in women in our culture. One manifestation of the distorted feminine is women blaming men for their unhappiness. These are often women who haven't confronted their passivity and dependency and considered that they are responsible for their own lives. I learned over time that my relationship pattern of trying to please was counterproductive. It exhausted me and rarely provided more than transitory happiness to any other who was looking to me for their happiness. These failed efforts in turn made me resentful.

Shortly before my illness, I began to meet women with strong and healthy feminine aspects. I saw in these new connections an availability of such qualities as nurturing, compassion, listening and intuition. Many of these women were also powerful in their communities and the world. I often saw in them a capacity for risk-taking, self-sufficiency and self-responsibility. Some of these women I met in the course of my everyday life and some are world teachers whose presentations or workshops I attended. I will describe several of them and the impact they had on me.

The first of these is Jean Houston, an author and master teacher of international renown. I first heard of Jean just after my marriage separation from a counselor who suggested I attend one of her workshops. He told me it would change my life. It did.

Jean is an interdisciplinarian with credentials in a wide spectrum of wisdom teachings, and a well-known leader in the human potential field. She speaks with great articulation, emotion and depth, and is fluent in several languages. In her youth she had lived with the anthropologist Margaret Mead and befriended the theologian Teilhard de Chardin. At the time of the workshop she was participating in experiments on human communication with dolphins. Jean is a large and vibrant woman who brings to mind the image of a Viking queen. When she speaks, her presence, dynamism and substance deeply affect her listeners.

Jean is an incredible original and so, naturally, her workshop was fascinating. In the first section of it – held in the ballroom of a New York hotel with several hundred of us participating – I found myself crawling on hands and knees or leaping about in an attempt to re-create various stages of evolution. In the course of the exercise, this still buttoned-up lawyer made the micro-movements of amoebae, and then lay flat as a flatworm on my belly. Fifteen minutes later, with the rest of the group, I found myself squatting and leaping on four legs in imitation of an early quadruped. This last part was amazingly energizing when I let loose and bound around the ballroom making jungle sounds like those of Tarzan's Cheetah. These sounds had lain hidden somewhere deep in my being waiting for the opportunity, finally, for expression. Not surprisingly, there were moments throughout the weekend when I felt like a fish out of water. I hoped the bar association was not taking photos of me, particularly in my simian character!

When the attendees were surveyed, less than five percent were doing work that was familiar to me. The participants included basket weavers, dancers, body workers, painters, sculptors, artists, writers – mostly people I might otherwise, at best, have made passing contact at a retail counter for tourists or a theater. My learning curve was high, and it was thrilling to be thrown into one new experience after the other.

One of the most memorable experiences came in the second part of the workshop, when Jean called on us to enact a Greek dream festival (aesclepian). For the last part of the celebration, we were to dress in white sheets and, at midnight, head into a large room to spend the night together sleeping on the floor. Our focus was to explore the meaning of miracles and dreams. Before going to sleep and to help in stimulating the mystic in our dreams, we were invited to share relevant true stories with each other.

Two of these still stand out. A woman told about being stranded on Mt. Shasta, the northern California mountain with mystical powers many have experienced. When an unexpected snowstorm arose, she lost her way. Panic set in; as nighttime approached, she feared that she would freeze to death. Suddenly a large bird appeared – she thought it might be a crow or a raven – and connected with her. She followed the bird and soon realized that it was leading her down the mountain to safety. When she finished the story, the gong rang and chills ran up my spine.

About fifteen years after hearing this story, I traveled to Mt. Shasta with Denise, my long-time girlfriend. I took a short hike into the mountains while she enjoyed herself in the shops on the main street. I was gone for twenty minutes when a huge storm erupted out of nowhere. Suddenly, I was caught in a torrential rain with streaks of lightning and roaring thunder. I was afraid of lightning, especially at these heightened elevations, and sought shelter in a nearby wooden shack. I was in the shack by myself only a few moments when the door opened and a Tibetan monk and his entourage in full robes entered. In this unexpected multicultural togetherness, we experienced a deep silence. The contrast between the roar of the thunder and our stillness, and the miracle of this happening at all, made it a sacred moment. This may have been the closest I would come to the Himalayas, squatting in a makeshift retreat on a sacred mountain with a Tibetan monk and his attendants. After I returned to the shopping district I asked Denise how she had experienced the storm. Surprised by my question she told me there hadn't been a storm; there hadn't even been a cloud in the sky. How different our experiences, only a short distance away.

The second story I recall from the dream fest belonged to Jean. She was vacationing with a group on a remote Greek isle, so remote that there was no radio contact and the next boat was not expected for days. She had cut herself on an underwater rock; the wound had become infected and began to worsen. She was afraid that gangrene might set in and she might lose a limb, or even her life, unless she got immediate medical attention. Hope was fading when, out of nowhere, a ship appeared on the horizon. To everyone's amazement, there was a doctor on board. This was not an ordinary doctor, but the Surgeon General of the United States; he gave Jean the needed medical attention. When Jean asked him how he came to be at this remote island, he explained he had offered his children a vacation anywhere in the world if they made their grades; they had chosen the Greek isles. The night before boarding, they decided to throw darts at a map to determine which island to explore. The dart landed on the remote island on which Jean and her group were stranded. She told us that without this miracle, she might not have survived.

While I don't remember my dreams from that night, I learned the next morning that similar dream patterns showed up in the people sleeping near each other. A number of people in one part of the room dreamed wild animals were chasing them, while in another they had romantic fantasies. But maybe the romantic fantasies had more to do with people rolling into each other through the night!

Jean had been experimenting with various forms of communication ranging from those transmitted through dreams to the ability of dolphins to communicate. And so, for the second experiment that week, we practiced sending messages into the Universe. We formed a personal thought or intent and channeled it upward through an imaginary cone into the cosmos. I couldn't help thinking of the Pink Floyd refrain, "Is anybody out there?"

Later we changed roles and became receptors, in case the Universe had any messages to return to us. To do this, we opened our imaginary cone with an intention to receive any communication that might want to come to us. I deflected my anxiety by joking with the person next to me that I might hear "the Yankees in seven." Actually, while in this mode of receptivity, I noticed that a large blob of purple in the shape of an eye began flashing in the center of my forehead. This flashing occurred sporadically for a year or more after the workshop. Even though I had no idea what the flashing eye meant, I enjoyed the experience. I felt I had made some connection with the great beyond. A couple of years later, I first heard the term "third eye," which refers to the psychic energy center located in the center of the forehead. According to the chakra, or energy center model that originated in the original yoga teachings of ancient India, the color of the third eye, the sixth chakra, is purple. This information made me consider that I might actually have made a nonverbal connection with something beyond this world.

Some years ago, I read a controversial report about Jean Houston that made the front page. She had served as an adviser to Hillary Rodham Clinton, then first lady, to help her work with some personal issues. Jean used an accepted therapeutic technique in asking Hillary to imagine the voice of her hero, Eleanor Roosevelt, offering advice to her on the questions on which she was reflecting. This was distorted by the media to look as if Jean had involved Hillary in a séance—talking with the dead. I assumed the distortion was planted by those who disliked the Clintons intensely. To me, criticizing someone for using Jean as an adviser was akin to criticizing a student for having Albert Einstein assist with a science project.

I was incensed. I could not understand what had happened to Jean and how this association, in which she had been asked to counsel one of the world's leading women, could be turned against her. In another context, and with a different use of language, it would be quite acceptable to have an imaginary conversation in which a deceased hero or absentee role model was asked for guidance. In sports, young men might be told by their football coach to imagine they heard the voice of Knute Rockne or a deceased teammate and to use that for motivation as they headed through the tunnel onto the football field.

Jean Houston is one of the most brilliant people I have had the privilege of meeting. She caused me to think globally and cosmically, and was the first person I knew who held a world view of humanity. Years later, when I participated in personal healings, I would always consider using our collective power to heal communal and global issues. Jean was the inspiration for that expanded view of what's possible. She continues to be a pioneer in envisioning a new world.

Another heroine of mine is teacher and author Marianne Williamson. I had been spending time with a friend in Los Angeles, focusing on regaining my health, when friends suggested I might like to attend Marianne's biweekly gatherings. Oprah Winfrey had promoted her book, *A Return to Love*, and she was enjoying great popularity. Several hundred seats filled quickly on the two nights each week that she spoke. I found these gatherings beautiful and inspirational. Marianne's expressions were clear and courageous. Her teachings were based on the book *A Course in Miracles*. As I understand it, the contents of *A Course in Miracles* were channeled from a higher source. A central thesis of those teachings was that in all situations we have only two choices: to act from love, or to act from fear.

Marianne often walked into the lecture hall with the AIDS support group with whom she had been meeting the previous hour. The group participants came into the room ready to integrate with the larger gathering. I felt this was a great example for humanity, to accept and assimilate those people most marginalized in the culture of that time. Marianne's work, explicitly and implicitly, addressed AIDS as a global issue, not just about those with the disease in this country, mostly gay men and drug users, who were often the objects of derision and fear.

At first, the contact with people with AIDS made me nervous. Neither I, nor anyone I knew, were in touch with those with AIDS. This was my first direct experience with the illness. I knew I needed to confront the fear, and I did, but I was embarrassed by my initial reluctance to mingle with those who were so ill. Later I wondered how much my rejection of these people, some of whom I came to know over time, was actually a rejection of my own unhealthy places and fear of death.

Unlike my image of the way spiritual teachers look, no rags or ash clothing hung from Marianne's shoulders. She wore designer clothes, red lipstick and was very attractive. I have since learned that spiritual teachers come in all shapes, degrees of wealth and egos. I've learned to listen to the messages instead of critiquing the dress or personalities of the messengers. I was once and for all disabused of the notion that spiritual teachers should look or act a particular way when I saw a turbaned yogi known for his deep compassion leave a workshop and drive away in a red Jaguar convertible. Wisdom arrives in different packages, cars and clothes, and I eventually came to welcome whoever most touched my heart.

At my first lecture, I had the current issue of *People* magazine on my lap and was sitting in an aisle seat when Marianne walked toward the podium. She was on the cover, and the article inside described her as "The Bitch of Love" because of some alleged problems in her interpersonal relationships. As she walked past, she looked at the magazine, tapped me on the shoulder and said lightly, "Don't believe everything you read!" She was tough-skinned, and I admired that.

My esteem for her has risen even more over the years. Her recent teachings have emphasized global issues, which I believe reflect her own shift from a focus on the personal to a macro-social approach. When I watched her on a television special with a group of politically-oriented participants in Washington, her response to their cold skepticism was to hold her ground and speak with her usual passion and directness. She never minced words or resorted to "weasel words" in her presentation. Before long, the audience appreciated that she was a woman of substance. I could see the respect for her grow as she spoke her truth.

A few years ago, I attended her speaking engagement in nearby Gainesville. My son Ben and his good friend Jay joined me, although I'm certain they would have preferred something more collegiate for the evening get-together. Marianne had the audience do a profoundly effective exercise she called "atonement", a way of saying we were sorry for wrongs committed and asking the aggrieved group or person for forgiveness.

The first atonement was directed to Native Americans. She asked that those of Native American descent stand. She then requested that a non-Native American stand and face each person already standing. Then she read a moving passage to be repeated by the non-Native American to the Native American while they looked into each other's eyes. The atonement detailed the atrocities and misdeeds committed toward the indigenous people of this country and offered the profound apologies of the one representing the offenders, followed by asking for forgiveness. The silence in the room was deafening. Once again, I experienced being in the presence of truth in community and its extraordinary power.

After the exercise was completed, one of the Native Americans rose to speak. With much emotion he told us that in all his years of hearing about the atrocities committed against his people, no one had ever apologized before, and that it meant a lot to him. The program continued with atonements offered to blacks and gays, and then between men and women. I was so glad that my son and his friend could witness these exchanges.

Marianne Williamson is a woman of great spiritual inventiveness, and we are fortunate she is one of those leading us into the new century. Thus, I was being exposed to women, those who had made their marks on the world independently of a man's status or connections. Their identities were self-derived through their own efforts and evolution and were not dependent on anyone else, whether or not they were married or in other intimate relationships. I found that most of these women also embodied a strong spiritual connection, which, in my healing explorations, had often brought me in contact with them. My experiences with what seemed like a new breed of women was to become instrumental in my healing process.

A third woman who deeply impacted me is Jeanette Jones. She took care of my mother during my mother's final four years. She has never received public attention, and certainly not prominence, in spite of her extraordinary deeds. We met shortly after my mother was diagnosed with cancer. My mother lived by herself, so Jeanette was coming to live with her on a full-time basis. In those first encounters, I was in an irritable mood. I was sick, had no energy and was self-absorbed. I also felt resentful about my mother's cancer. Underneath my irritation was the devastation of knowing that I would be losing her. Whatever the excuse, my moods were lousy and I wasn't easy to get along with.

Jeanette's attitude was remarkable. She embodied and expressed optimism and joy on even the darkest days and also expressed gratitude to those around her regularly. Jeanette woke up in the room next to my mother's, singing. I wondered why she was so happy when her job required her to spend her days taking care of a sick woman. How could this be a day to look forward to? I noticed, with some guilt, that she seemed happier on a bad day than I did on a good one. Her singing reminded me of the great West African percussion genius Baba Olatunje, when he would play his drums and sing a beautiful African song, which, he told us, translated, as "it's great to be alive." Like Olatunje, Jeanette's roots were in Africa, but flavored by her southern upbringing.

Over time, Jeanette and my mother became best friends. Their relationship transcended that of employer/employee. They were totally different in appearance and style, yet they traveled everywhere together, from the hairdresser down the street to the Ritz Carlton in Naples, Florida, for my mother's annual birthday gathering. Jeanette was a large, wide woman with pearly white teeth and a big smile. My mother, by comparison, was now pale and thin, although she was feisty and classy. Mom often reminded me of the mature Katharine Hepburn. It was a sad and touching day when Mom went into the final stage of dying. Jeanette had taken her to the hairdresser and, when they got home, Mom was unable to get out of the car. I watched from the window as Jeanette picked Mom up in her arms and then, walking into the house, heralded their return by announcing, "Make way for Mrs. Fink." When Mom died, Jeanette mourned as deeply as her life-long friends. Even now, she will tell me time and again when something reminds her of my mother and how much she misses her.

Jeanette went through an extremely difficult period when her son, Jeffrey, a preacher in his thirties, had a sudden stroke without warning and was paralyzed from the neck down. Jeanette worked her day job and then sat in the various hospitals with Jeffrey until all hours of the night, praying for a miracle. He almost died several times, but miraculously survived and lives near her today. She also lost her husband to Alzheimer's disease during this same period. I attended his funeral, a glorious celebration in Black Southern Baptist style with celebratory singing and musical accompaniment. The minister, wearing a gold necklace and chains, walked down the aisle touching people with healing gestures. If it's possible to have a good time at a funeral, this was it. People were singing and dancing in the aisles in celebration of the man's life.

I do not often experience Jeanette's easygoing attitude and ebullient optimism, but I knew I needed a good dose of whatever she had, which I believe was one reason she was brought into my life. I am happy that such a heartfelt person will be among those who take us into the new century, not by fame, but by the way she leads her life.

The fourth woman I add to this list is Lucy Rivers McCartney. I consider Lucy my original spiritual teacher, as she provided me with profound guidance at the beginning of my illness. I met Lucy when I was still practicing as an attorney; she was a massage therapist. She practiced out of the back room of a recreational center in a swinging singles apartment complex. The sacredness of her massage room was in marked contrast to the faint beat of the disco I could hear through the walls. I was approaching the end of my marriage, which had taken on destructive overtones, and these massage sessions allowed me to express all the things I was experiencing and to hear her guidance.

As with many men, the only person with whom I exchanged emotional intimacies at that time was my wife. When our problems escalated, I found myself emotionally isolated. In turning to Lucy, I experienced a brand of wisdom far deeper than what I would have expected of a woman eleven years my junior. She spoke of higher principles and divine guidance, and on a practical level stressed how important it was that I take care of my body. She also taught yoga and meditation, which were totally unknown to me before I met her.

I initially felt guilty breaking away from my law practice in the middle of the day for these clandestine massage rendezvous, which I considered self-indulgent at the time. Now I see them as acts of self-love. I soon noticed that many of the prominent businessmen from town would show up at her place, including the mayor and the city's best-known businessman and his family. This convinced me that something extraordinary was happening, and I soon let go of my guilt for taking time off.

My marriage had turned acrimonious. Although I understood that I was a party to the conflicts, I had no understanding of how to make it any different. Lucy suggested that I read Ken Keyes' *Handbook to*

Higher Consciousness for help. I read it while flying with my wife to Washington, D.C. I was a white-knuckle flyer, and that day had a couple of martinis to numb my fears. The handbook described a ladder of stages of spiritual development; in all candor, I felt I could at least be at mid-level on the scale. When the martinis started talking, I optimistically raised my estimate. But when I came upon yet another passage, it was such a shock to me that I couldn't hold onto my martini. I blurted out to my wife that I was at the bottom rung, which is about power, sex and money. I laughed on the outside but cringed on the inside, because I knew I had a long way to go. To end up a bottom-dweller on the scale of higher consciousness meant I was misdirected rather than failing for lack of effort. Accepting that revelation was a huge step. Only then could I consciously change direction, since awareness is the necessary precondition for change.

I was impressed with how Lucy was handling her own divorce. One day she told me that two people who had just left her massage room were the husband who she was divorcing and his "new woman," as she casually put it. I figured the meeting was about dividing assets, but she told me she was counseling them one at a time during massage sessions.

Lucy also had a new man in her life, Ron, who had extraordinary skills, energy and humor; she would later marry him, and he and I would become close friends. Lucy told me how important it was to leave her marriage in a good place; to my amazement, she performed the wedding ceremony when her ex-husband remarried, and was named godmother of his first child. I thought that if someone could pull this off, then there really was hope for me in a primary relationship.

Ron was a carpenter and had built a sailboat, which they named *Sunshine*, on which they lived. One Monday night, I heard through a mutual friend that they were traveling on *Sunshine* and were scheduled to tie up at a marina in St. Augustine, only 30 miles away. I drove there after work, hoping to surprise them. They didn't show up, and they had no way to know I had been looking for them. The following Friday, I received an unexpected letter from Lucy dated the morning after I had gone to the marina. She wrote that she had seen me in her dreams and described my journey in detail and with remarkable accuracy. She thanked me for being so open that such "dream communication could happen."

The letter floored me. I had been interested in her feedback about what I had been doing and had asked the question silently to myself. But she heard me in her dreams the evening I had looked for her, and responded by letter as casually as if I had left a message on her answering machine.

A number of experiments have confirmed by empirical means the validity of alternative forms of communication. One is the widely published report about an experiment measuring the effect of prayer on people undergoing surgery. The study showed that the people who were prayed for did better during their surgery and recuperated faster than those in a control group who were not prayed for. None of the participants knew whether or not they would be the subject of prayer.

My daughter Julie is particularly receptive to higher intelligence and non-physical forms of communication. When she was a child, I had purchased a white Great Pyrenees puppy from Minnesota that was to be flown to Florida the next day. We had talked about possible names for it but had gone to bed without choosing one. The next morning Julie, then a young child, told me when she woke up that she had a name for the puppy. "Let's name him Casper," she announced. "It came to me in the night." I called the owner of the kennel a few minutes later to confirm that the plane had departed on time, and asked if they had named the puppy. She told me she had, in fact, named the puppy Casper. Since Great Pyrenees are usually white, and the cartoon character Casper the Ghost is white, I asked if that was a common name for that breed of dog. The kennel owner replied it was the only Casper she had heard of during her many years in the business.

Julie has also intuited on several occasions that I was not well, and once located me in a motel in Massachusetts on one of my most difficult nights, without any factual knowledge on her part that I was in trouble. Julie continues in my life as the glue that binds, contacting me almost daily by phone and having contact with all branches of the family, siblings, parents, in-laws and grandparents in addition to having an active and fun-filled life with her husband Jeff, a man of unbriddled enthusiasm and creativity. This same intuition brings her into easy and close relationships with people from diverse backgrounds and with a variety of belief systems, in both her personal and professional life, where she has served as a public defender and a lawyer to families with children involved in dependency hearings. I am grateful not only that she has this gift, but that she has the will and perseverance to use it in such a positive way.

My long-time girlfriend Denise is also very receptive to communications not of this world. She has been an oncology nurse for more than twenty years and has often worked with the dying with great compassion. Her patients and their families often want her at bedside during their time of dying. Because of this closeness, she will sometimes have visitations from her patients who have passed over. Many years ago, we went to Cassadega, a psychic community in central Florida. In a reading with a clairvoyant, a number of her patients spoke to her; the clairvoyant stated the name or identifying initials of each before delivering the message.

Lucy always talked to me about my personal presence and attention. I was so distracted in my fast-paced legal life that I often did things reflecting my lack of awareness. I once found my briefcase on fire after putting it on the kitchen drain board when I got home from work. I hadn't noticed that an edge was touching the burner. Then, when it went up in flames, I burned my hand putting out the fire! It caused quite a stir the next day when I walked down the office corridors carrying a charred briefcase.

Another time, a senior partner asked me, during a conference with a client, why I was so exacting about time. I looked down and to my embarrassment saw that I was wearing two watches, and it only increased my embarrassment when I noticed that they were both on the same wrist.

These cases of non-presence were not solely my personal province. My brother, Neal, also a lawyer, forgot where he had parked his car one day and reluctantly returned home without it. Another example of attorney absentmindedness occurred during my early years of practice. A senior partner, Earl, had requested that a young associate, Steve, carry Earl's briefcases to the front of the building after work. Earl was to stop by in his sports car and pick up his briefcases on the way home. I waited with Steve for about 25 minutes, when a five-minute wait should have sufficed. We were worried and decided to call Earl's house to see what had happened. His wife answered the phone and informed us that everything was fine. Earl had just finished dinner and was beginning his dessert, having forgotten Steve and his bag. Steve would later command a high position in the Florida House of Representatives, and ultimately lose the election for governor in the last several days, but on this day he was a lowly associate who was left holding the bag in more ways than one.

Probably my most absentminded tale comes from the time when Ron and Lucy, having arrived at my house while I was away, left some heart-shaped candies on the kitchen counter before going out again. When I returned, I felt antsy and proceeded to eat most of the candies. Lucy soon came back accompanied by her dog; a cocker spaniel named Aggie, and asked me where I had put Aggie's food. When I asked, surprised, "What food?" she told me it was the heart-shaped candies she had left in the kitchen. Backed into a corner, I reluctantly confessed to eating the dog food. But I was not off the hook with this. She then asked what I had done with the large heartworm pill that had been sitting in the middle of the candy. I sheepishly confessed a second time; I had also downed the dog's heartworm pill. My embarrassment was quickly overshadowed by concern for my digestive tract, along with the irregular palpitations that kept beat to the conversation.

The busier I became, the more exaggerated my tendency toward absentmindedness. When I learned yoga and meditation, this began to change. These practices kept me centered in one place, more or less, but only if I took the time to do them.

I came to realize that only in allowing the feminine into my life could I turn these patterns around. It was through the four women I've described, along with Denise, my daughters Julie and Allison, Ben's long-time girlfriend Samantha and all the others who modeled sensitivity with depth and focus with heart, that I began to consider how much I had abdicated the feminine within myself. That awareness, inevitably, would lead to a happier and healthier balance in me. I would become softer, more available, and more heart-centered. At the same time, the qualities of focus and calm sense of direction would release the obsessive drive that ultimately sent me to my sickbed.

Unbuttoned / Ken Fink

Chapter Eight

MY MOTHER FACES DEATH

"The greatest discovery of any generation is that
human beings can alter their lives by altering
the attitudes of their minds."
ALBERT SCHWEITZER

Unbuttoned / Ken Fink

*I*n 1985, while I was still struggling with my own illness, her doctors told my mother that her diagnosis of cancer was terminal. They gave her six months to live. As it turned out, she actually survived an additional four years.

It annoyed me that doctors would declare someone "terminal." We're all terminal in the sense that we're all in the process of dying. I felt that only the patients should decide for themselves if they were going to die soon. Dr. Deepak Chopra, among other physicians who have spoken and written about life and death, has told many stories about patients outliving the very doctors who had pronounced them terminal.

Considering my mother's serious medical diagnosis, we felt we had some freedom to experiment with different healing modalities. I believed she could definitely prolong her life and, in the process, become empowered in her own process of self-healing. None of what we would explore was toxic or uncomfortable.

Immediately after her diagnosis, I took her to a doctor who used only natural medicines, along with a technique called "applied kinesiology" to test the strength of her various body systems and organs. He gave her vitamins and supplements, which she felt strengthened her greatly. I also brought carrot juice, shitake mushrooms and shark cartilage capsules to her on my daily visits. At the same time, I sat by her bed and took my own supplements, to make this a shared experience. She was pleased with my offerings and I with her receptivity, and she found hope in these new treatments. This was in sharp contrast to the process of chemotherapy she had undergone, which seemed to leave her passive and disempowered. She'd had no participation through that process beyond waiting for the treatments and, afterwards, for the results of the various tests and scans which indicated how effective–or not–the treatments had been.

Over the next four years, she told me repeatedly of her conviction that her unexpected longevity after the diagnosis was the result of the new therapies with which she worked. I believe the attention she was receiving from my brother Neal, his wife, Jean, her five grandchildren, and her friends also contributed significantly to her additional years. Julie, with whom Mom had a special relationship, was particularly attentive and would telephone her daily and fly down from Brandeis University in Boston as often as she could to be with her and have their special times together. Between the personal support and the therapies, her willingness to fight for her life was greatly enhanced. Because those who were helping her strongly believed she could be helped, she had a wonderful support group with which to share her successes. The time we spent with her turned into a real deepening of our relationship with her.

I felt badly that I had not spent more time with my mother before she became ill, but was happily making up for that now. We sat together in the evening and often reminisced about the past. We regaled in laughter over one story she told; so familiar it was in terms of the way I had been. Her house alarm had gone off early one morning and, worried, she telephoned me at the office. I immediately called the alarm company, which said they would send someone to her house at once, and then I told her I'd call back shortly to make sure she was all right. About fourteen hours later, still at my desk – I was under a lot of pressure around a securities offering that day – I suddenly remembered with a sinking feeling that I had totally forgotten her. I immediately dialed the phone, which she answered with: "Good thing I wasn't depending on you," and then, lest I get off too easily, reminded me that she could have long been dead if a killer had been in the house.

My mother had limits to what types of alternative therapies she would try. When the chemotherapy treatments proved to be ineffective, I looked into clinics in Mexico that were using laetrile, which was banned in the U.S. but getting hopeful reports from some quarters. One regimen consisted of using laetrile, eating a vegetarian diet, and taking coffee enemas and mega doses of vitamins. A few years earlier I had met a former business executive, very "non-alternative," who told me that laetrile treatment had dissolved his tumor, which had been the size of a baseball and considered untreatable by his doctors (he at one time was written up as a miracle cure in the Celestine Prophecy News Letter). But when I showed my mother a video of the work being done at a recommended Mexican clinic, it was the only time during the course of her disease I saw her fearful. She said she would rather do nothing than go to a Mexican clinic. I never knew exactly what it was that upset her, but I dropped the subject immediately.

By the spring of 1989, the cancer had spread to my mother's lungs. In addition to dealing with cancer, she had fallen and broken her hip. She started to give away her jewelry and was clearly relinquishing her will to live. I felt helpless. I had always believed it was my responsibility to solve the problems of the women in my life, but now I could do nothing about her declining health, which was deeply disturbing to me. Then, on Mother's Day, Denise told me that a group of Philippine psychic surgeons were in town. These healers rarely came to the United

States, and I was surprised they were in my hometown and actually doing healing in a nearby home.

I had heard about the psychic surgery done in the Philippines and how it was reputed in that culture to result in medical miracles. When I looked into this form of healing for my mother, and myself I knew I was experimenting with something that I had no evidence would be helpful. But, while there were clearly no assurances, at this point there didn't seem to be much to lose. All I knew was that psychic surgeons claimed to be able to enter the body with their hands and without an incision. While that seemed pretty unlikely to me, someone I respected a great deal had taken his sick wife to the Philippines, and after traveling with several psychic surgeons for a year, swore by the efficacy of their treatments. I had mentioned these healers to my mother a couple of years earlier, but since it meant traveling to the Philippines, she wasn't interested. When I asked her if she would let them treat her now, she said that she would only if they came to her house, which didn't make it easy for me.

I decided to go to an evening of healings. When I drove up to the house, there were so many cars that it looked like a high school football game. It was evident that people had traveled there from places near and far. Inside, dozens of people were gathered, squeezed in the best they could. Each person had arrived with his or her illness, holding a unique hope for healing. When the healer, Mart, came into the living room, he silently pointed to the person he was going to work with next. There was no sign-up sheet, and no visible order of treatment had been established. My expectation that people be treated on a first-come, first-served basis was irrelevant; I knew I needed to relax into this new protocol. The chosen person followed Mart into a back room and returned five to ten minutes later, his treatment completed. I am not particularly patient, and the endless wait tested my limits. I wound up sitting in the living room for twelve hours and was never called. I went home that evening quite frustrated.

Unwilling to give up, I returned early the next morning with Denise. About 100 people had already shown up. While we waited, a uniformed policeman told us that Mart had just taken his eyeball out of its socket, cleaned it, and then returned it. There were many other amazing stories, all of which defied my belief system. Some of the hopefuls had not been healed by traditional medicine; others had not sought traditional treatment; and probably some could not afford traditional treatment. Perhaps I expected to see a bunch of desperate kooks; instead, I was looking at a representative cross-section of the community no different than what I might find in the supermarket. When discussions arise about psychic surgeons, there is always the question about whether or not what they do is a fraud. Some years before, a television series came to the conclusion that these healers were unquestionably charlatans. This was at a time when there was an even greater bias than there is today against nontraditional healing therapies. In assessing alternative therapies, a representative medical doctor was usually called upon to report to the public his opinion about the legitimacy of the therapy. This is like having a Republican tell you if a Democrat is doing a good job, or vice-versa. The bias of the commentators disturbed me. I wanted these health systems to be autonomous and have their own methods of evaluation. We can always anticipate the likelihood that traditional medicine isn't going to put its stamp of approval on alternative medicine; if it did, it probably would not be a generous stamp. These treatments needed to be judged by different standards, by different people, and from a different perspective.

Whenever the results of medical research are reported and they're surprising or shocking in any respect, I first question who commissioned the study. This is rarely disclosed and, human nature being what it is, I am skeptical of studies funded by organizations that have an agenda, whether or not the study itself claims to be independent. I had found in the business world that if an independent business or real estate appraisal was needed to support the dollar value of a transaction, one could usually find an "independent" appraiser who would arrive at that exact dollar value or more. I wondered if medical research worked the same way. The testing organization might not be funded again if the sponsor failed to get the results that supported its agenda.

During this same period, segments of the traditional medical community made charges that chiropractors were frauds. But speak to a medical doctor with chronic neck or back problems and he is likely to be using a chiropractor. Chiropractors now receive more visits from people with neck and back pain than do traditional doctors.

I did not experience psychic surgery as fraudulent, although the experience, in many respects, far exceeded my belief system and, in retrospect, still seems strange.

I've seen that people typically lock into their positions. The more you defend something new or untested, the more it's challenged. When I was a kid, I listencd to medical professionals testify that there was no proof that cigarette smoking was dangerous to your health, and that such allegations were unsubstantiated. Then came the extended period when it was reported that cigarette smoking might be implicated in lung cancer, but there was no proof that smoking impacted other cancers or diseases. We were told that without "proof" smoking was harmful, it was safe to continue smoking. I reasoned that if it took twenty years to convince people that cigarette smoking was harmful– in spite of the obvious fact that it caused coughing and sputtering, and autopsies showed the lungs of smokers to be black and tarred – how could these same people be convinced of the validity of psychic surgery, which was much more tenuous?

There was no fixed price for Mart's services, but we were asked to make voluntary contributions. The amount suggested was not excessive by any standard. It was my impression that he and his assistants worked with great energy and passion and weren't doing this work for the money. They worked incredible hours and finished the day only when they were ready to drop from exhaustion. They also worked nonstop for several weeks at a time and then took a break for complete relaxation, like military personnel assigned to an isolated duty station. I've been told they believe that their psychic surgery gift is their sacred calling, and that if they don't use their gift they will die prematurely.

I had been waiting on the second day for about ten minutes, prepared to stay the full day, when Mart came out and pointed to me. When I went back to the room with him, it was full of people, including those who were videotaping the healing. I usually came to my traditional doctors with my written list of symptoms so that I wouldn't forget anything. However, Mart wasn't interested in symptoms and took no notes. Instead, he followed his intuition to the places on the body that needed healing. After I was on the table about ten minutes, I felt Mart's hands enter my abdomen. Throughout the procedure, fears were racing through my mind. I worried about the possibility of infection or the transmission of disease. I finally calmed down by telling myself that if God granted such extraordinary powers to a few select people, it was unlikely this process would kill me. After his foray into my abdomen, I pointed to my forehead; I wanted him to open my psychic intuitive center. He worked in that area for a few minutes but happily stayed outside the body. After leaving the table, I felt balanced and peaceful.

Later that day, Denise watched Mart remove cysts from her mother's breasts. Another person, a former state legislator, told me that Mart had cured his impotence (this was in the pre-Viagra days). One friend, a woman from New York who went to South America for a healing ceremony for her breast cancer, told me that the psychic surgeon on hand suddenly started working on a woman who was in the audience as a spectator. Afterwards, they all learned she was being treated for cancer, which he diagnosed on the spot. He didn't ask for her HMO card or a referral from her primary physician, he just went at it. These talented healers are reputed to be able to do their work without the surgery, but they enter the body because people don't otherwise believe they are healed. We seem to require blood and guts to believe that healing has really taken place.

My primary mission here actually concerned my mother, but I was told that Mart wouldn't treat anybody outside this particular house. Even though it was a long shot – "nothing ventured, nothing gained" – at the end of the day I grabbed Mart's arm and asked him if he would come to my mother's house. To my great joy and surprise, and even though he had declined all other home visits, he nodded.

Then he saw my mother. Afterwards, he took me into the next room and told me, sadly, that he wouldn't be able to cure her. I asked him to proceed with the healing, anyway, and do what he could.

My mother had never acknowledged a belief in a higher power. She went to services and did the proper things around religious holidays, but a belief in God had not been a cornerstone of her life and was remote from her everyday reality. In spite of this fact, we formed a prayer circle around my mother's bed. In this circle were Mart, the psychic surgeon; his Philippine nurse; Denise, an Interdenominational Christian; my mother's caretaker Jeanette a southern Baptist; one of Jeanette's friends; and myself. I felt that the diverse makeup of this healing circle was itself a healing. My mother had fraternized throughout her life with women of her own class and background and was a bit snobbish, and I noted with humor that this was not the most likely group to be found at her bridge table. I was moved by the whole experience.

When Mart first touched my mother, who was then almost blind from macular degeneration and expecting only surface touching, she gasped, "You didn't say he was going to cut me!" I reassured her that there wouldn't be any actual incision or pain, but Jeanette, who was watching, still screamed, as he appeared to enter her abdomen with his bare hand. He then removed some tissue, which he said was cancerous, and fixed a hernia for which she had previously been advised to have surgery. Next he moved his fingers between her physical eyes and worked on her third eye, her spiritual center. This seemed to be the most important part of this work.

In the days that followed, I could see that my mother was changed by this experience. For one thing, she expressed a belief that there was some greater power, the first time I had ever heard her say that. For the remaining two months of her life – an unexpected gift I believe was related to this healing work – she had greater acceptance and less struggle with her approaching death. She had lain flat on her back for some weeks since breaking her hip, but the day after the healing, she sat up. On the following day, she stood up; one day later, she ordered a wheel chair ramp built, and then jauntily headed off to keep her previously scheduled doctor's appointment.

I felt high from my experience with the Philippine healer and went for a walk the next day just as the sun was rising along the beach. But my exhilaration was short-lived when I came upon the body of a dead businessman, who I later learned had been bludgeoned to death by a prostitute. He was dressed in a suit and lay on a nearby beach access. I arrived on the scene only minutes after the police.

What did this mean, I asked myself? I felt the polarities of the Universe at work. Several hours earlier I had experienced the presence of a unique healing power. Now, I was in the presence of darkness. I recalled that I had asked the psychic surgeon to open my vision and I guess it had opened to everything – darkness as well as light.

Several years later, I had another experience of light and darkness in close proximity in time and space. I had been among thousands of people who had come to hear the Dalai Lama speak. I had trouble understanding his English and absorbing the substance of what he was saying, but found the energy emanating from him to be extraordinary and illuminating. I was energized and feeling high when I left the gathering. When I returned to my expressway motel, I called the adjacent restaurant to order a hamburger. Ten minutes later, I walked next door to pick up my food and found several people wounded by gunshots lying outside the restaurant. I was told that a drug deal had gone bad and the dealer had chased these people into the restaurant and then shot them. Here it was again: the high energy of the Dalai Lama and the dark energy of a drug deal gone bad, the light and the dark of the Universe, only three hours apart.

I tried to understand what had actually transpired with Mart's healing. There was a long lineage of fine physicians in my family, skillful, heartfelt and dedicated people, cut somewhat from the Marcus Welby image each of whom I trusted implicitly. I reasoned that my radical departure from that form of medicine into this alternative domain, while strange, came about because I had no other choice. But what Mart had done in the course of his surgeries clearly went beyond the boundaries of my belief system. I felt unequivocally that healing had taken place and that a godly intent to heal was at work. How it happened was beyond my ability to understand. If medicine didn't understand how aspirin worked, did I really want to get hung up on the "how?" Maybe this was simply another case of a multi-dimensional reality that we can only attempt to describe in two-dimensional terms.

What proof do we seek to ascertain if healing has taken place? Did we need to look at x-rays or blood tests to determine that a healing had occurred for my mother, or merely acknowledge that she went from deteriorating to improving as quickly as a basketball point guard running a fast break.

We need different methods to prove the validity of occurrences beyond our normal understanding. If thousands of people witness the statue of Mother Mary with tears rolling down her cheeks, should we take this as proof that it happened, or do we have to validate these events by having a chemist check for sodium where the tears emanate from the marble? If we were confronted with a creature with a green face and big ears who floated to earth without an airplane, would we stick a thermometer up his rectum and take his blood pressure to make certain he was real?

I read in the newspaper a few years ago, in an article so small and hidden that it was almost unnoticeable, that scientists now considered the Universe to be twice as old as they had believed the day before. If proof of the age of the Universe can be off by 100 percent, what other so-called facts will be proven wrong some day? In the last dozen or so years, it's been incontrovertibly shown that the bacteria H.pylori causes certain peptic ulcers. Several years before, when I asked a gastroenterologist if ulcers could be caused by bacteria, he assured me that it was impossible and laughed at the antibacterial remedies I was taking from a natural health practitioner. Sadly, a common disease had been mistreated by Western medicine for the better part of a century, although the accepted treatment had been scientifically proven.

I understood that my experience with psychic surgery would be difficult to describe to my friends and relatives. If I recounted the story to them, I expected they would either go silent or attack the credibility of my experience, which I was having a problem understanding myself—much less defending. Shirley MacLaine had written about her experience with the psychic surgeons who had stayed at her house in Malibu, where they performed numerous healings. Her report matched my experience very closely. I found it irritating to be constantly challenged about something I had found to be quite profound but had difficulty explaining.

Before my mother passed, there was one interchange that was of particular importance to me. I had told her many times that I would miss her. Each time she would respond, "Miss me, don't mourn me." During her last week, I sat with her every evening at 5:00 p.m., which had always been the cocktail hour for her and my father, who had died seventeen years earlier. They would sit together after he got home from work and share a Whitehorse scotch and soda. This was a particularly happy time during my growing up years, as I would often join them during this hour to visit and rehash the day. Now I revived that ritual, telling her of my day and having a scotch for both of us. She was unable to speak but listened while I talked. I was already mourning her loss and sometimes tears flowed down my cheeks during this sweet time of communion. I was sad for myself but happy for her, because I knew she wanted to be released from her suffering.

Still, I felt incomplete because she had never said anything about missing me. We had been in this long fight for life together and I knew I would experience a period of emptiness after she was gone. So one night I whispered to my silent mother, believing she couldn't hear me, "Mom, are you going to miss me?" At that very moment, after not having said anything for hours, she sat straight up in her bed, put her arms around my neck, and told me, "I miss you already." In that moment, I felt that the two of us had completed our earth journey together.

Two nights later, Jeanette called us into the bedroom to say that Mom was about to pass. A few minutes later, she took one gasp that appeared to be her last and then, thirty seconds later, her final breath.

Afterwards, I sat with her, alone, before the hospice agency was called. In this time I played recordings of Sanskrit chants and prayed. My father had passed away in the same room from a heart attack, and my family of origin had experienced many profound moments in this room. I was aware that my time to feel comforted and supported here had come to an end.

The next morning, I took my three children to the nursing home to tell my grandmother that my mother, her last surviving child had died. Needless to say, it was painful to deliver this information to my ninety-eight-year-old grandmother, whom I loved dearly. Even when prepared for the inevitable, it is still difficult.

Several months later my brother, Neal, and I sat on the floor of my mother's house dividing up her personal possessions. We flipped a coin for who chose first. It was curious that we used the family rules for dividing things that we had learned as young children, flipping a coin and then alternating choices. This was our family way of being fair. I thought, momentarily, that perhaps we could informally see who needed what, but we never considered doing it any other way. I had moved to that house when I was ten years old and it was now thirty-four years later. It was a place where I had always been welcome and treated as special, a place of shelter and comfort, and this was its final hour.

My mother had left me an inheritance, which enabled me to continue with my healing journey and meet my financial obligations. This made a huge difference when my personal health deteriorated shortly afterwards, and again I found myself flat on my back. I'd invited my son and a friend to Western Massachusetts to share a cabin I had rented for a month, but I found that after a couple of weeks I needed to send them home and once again focus solely on my recovery. I had looked forward to our time together but there was nothing else I could do. Denise took off work and came up to New England to help me in my recovery. She is one of the world's great nurturers and used her healing strengths to revive me and help me prepare for the next step. At that time she introduced me to the powerful work of author and theologian Catherine Ponder and her teachings about the power of prayer, which I used for years to help me through difficult times.

I was referred to a spiritual adviser in Saratoga Springs, New York, who was recommended for being particularly talented at offering guidance about healing the body. I came to rely on Marina Petro's counseling for many years on a variety of issues. She described a place of healing that would be good for me, but could not name it or say where it was. She had seen a row of trees leading up a long drive to a formidable looking building at the top of a hill. Wondering how I might locate this place with such incomplete information, I decided to try describing Marina's vision to people in the area; I was then staying for a short time in Western Massachusetts. I soon learned that the description perfectly matched the healing center founded by Dr. Deepak Chopra, then located in Lancaster, Massachusetts, only a three-hour drive away. Dr. Chopra was then known mostly by the holistic healing community and was just beginning to gain national prominence through his new book, *Quantum Healing.*

The two-week program in which I enrolled was expensive, but I felt at the end that I had gotten my money's worth. The experience introduced me to the ancient Indian medical system of Ayurveda, a natural system of healing that had been used successfully over thousands of years. I found it persuasive that Dr. Chopra, a distinguished endocrinologist in Boston, focused instead on the Ayurvedic tradition in his health center.

The Ayurvedic system seeks to bring the entire body back into a natural balance rather than focusing on any single part or disease system. The physician takes several pulses, not just one, then examines the tongue, skin coloring, and other external factors. From this, he diagnoses the patient as one of three body types or doshas: pitta, vata or kapha. Pitta represents fire, vata represents air, and kapha represents water and earth. The diagnosis includes identifying which of these elements are out of balance.

I was told that I had excessive vata, or too much air. This meant I was prone to too much whirling mental activity and not enough grounding. I was treated with different foods, oils, scents and herbs, all directed toward my particular imbalance. I was told to eat root vegetables and avoid airy foods such as popcorn, and refined sesame oil was applied to my skin. I was also advised to use ginger for taste. Meditation and gentle colonics were both essential parts of the treatment. Particularly enjoyable were the panchakarma massage treatments, for which I was dressed in a loincloth and then rolled in a vat of oil.

Another treatment involved dripping oil slowly on the middle of my forehead, while another involved two people, or four hands, working on me in unison. One would take my right arm and the other my left and together rub oil into my arms in synchronized movements. I was reminded of the Tin Man, Scarecrow and Lion from *The Wizard of Oz*, who were buffed up in unison by the Wizard's helpers before their visit to the Great Wizard. I wondered if there would be a Great Wizard in my future. While these treatments seemed bizarre and actually humorous by my erstwhile standards, I slowly recovered. After two weeks, I again felt my life force return; I was ready for what was next. I used Ayurveda for only short-term assistance, but it was exactly what I needed.

Chapter Nine

SYNCHRONICITY

"The most incomprehensible thing about the
universe is that it is comprehensible."
ALBERT EINSTEIN

Unbuttoned / Ken Fink

*I*n determining which path I would follow at any given time, a number of markers inexplicably appeared and pointed to the same direction. Some might label this merely a coincidence; others would contend that there are no coincidences. I found that if the convergence of events made energetic sense, either by giving me an experience of high energy or a feeling of divine guidance, it was usually a blessing. This was the Universe's way of pointing to a new direction for me. I don't have any idea how this happens, but I do know there is intelligence behind it. Whenever I've paid attention to certain things appearing in my life, often unexpectedly, it has led to something meaningful and helpful, at times extraordinarily so. I once heard a speaker suggest our conscious connection to the Universe can be measured by the extent to which we pay attention to synchronistic events and don't dismiss them as coincidence.

Throughout my journey, there have been a number of instances in which a synchronicity of events unveiled a new direction for me. These sometimes happened when I was feeling most lost, as if I were in an airplane circling endlessly in the dark. Then, suddenly, a lighted runway would appear and point the way. Some of these instances occurred dramatically and others in the normal course of my life.

One of the first happened just prior to my divorce and before my illness. I was at the Jean Houston workshop described earlier, and Jean arranged for the group to have a "primal experience" together. Half of the group would be blindfolded; they would dance to drum music inside a circle formed by the other half.

When the recording of *Drums of Passion* rhythmically boomed into the night, I was struck by the coincidence that I was hearing the West African drumming performance that had been my favorite since my early twenties— music not known by many. I was dancing blindfolded for ten minutes when I found myself passionately kissing a woman who was also blindfolded. I felt uninhibited, loose and free. But I was also surprised, especially since this exercise was not designed to be an interaction between men and women. And, of course, there arose the inevitable question: whom was I kissing?

After the dance, I continued to hold the woman's hand; I knew that if I let it go, I might lose her in the crowd and never discover her identity. When we finally removed our blindfolds, I found myself with a petite, attractive blonde who laughed a lot and had great energy. We exchanged names – hers was Ellen – and I asked where she lived. When she answered, "Jacksonville, Florida," chills went up my spine. My hometown! I was a thousand miles from home and had mysteriously connected with the only other Floridian in a group of ninety people through a passionate kiss while blindfolded. As we talked about our backgrounds and circumstances, the coincidences mounted. We had both been married for fourteen years and had recently separated. Her husband had moved to the same small beach community where I was living. I also discovered that she and her husband had attended the same university as me, and at the same time.

After we returned home, we spent a few intense evenings together, which then segued into a phone friendship over the next few years. This brief encounter with a woman was one of the first after my separation and would lead to important realizations for me. What were the lessons learned from this synchronistic meeting? There were two. Through our conversations about our respective divorces, I came to understand how victimized Ellen felt by her ex. I was able to see that I, too, had assumed a victim role in my divorce; Ellen helped me break that pattern. I also saw, for the first time, that my intense, passionate fire belonged to me, alone, and was not sourced by anyone else. I had often attributed my sensual and sexual passion to my female partners. Through being with Ellen, I discovered that that lusty appetite was mine and would accompany me wherever I ventured. In my astrological chart, I have the Sun, Moon, Mercury and Venus all in the fire sign of Aries, so intensity and passion are written in the stars for me. It was a breakthrough to finally realize the truth of that, and celebrate it.

One of my most life-altering synchronicities occurred in the early 90s while I was on the massage table of a friend, a massage therapist named Steve, in Lenox, Massachusetts. That day he told me, frankly, he thought the physical conditions about which I complained were unconscious manifestations to put me in touch with all the healers and healing modalities I found so fascinating. He suggested that I consider enrolling in a healing school. "Maybe you can learn about what fascinates you directly, instead of through illness," he said.

Steve had personally mastered many different healing systems. He had expertise in massage, energy healing and the Option Process (a dialogue therapy). He was also skilled in reflexology and acupressure and was teaching a connective tissue course at a leading massage school. In addition to enjoying the bodywork, I loved Steve's company. His buoyant optimism and boundless energy, plus his eagerness to explore the great beyond, inspired me. He was highly motivated in his search for meaning and would pursue his areas of expertise with no holds barred. At the same time, he was quite grounded in the physical world, ran a successful business with his wife and was responsible with his obligations. When we were together we often talked about the mysteries of the Universe and shared our own personal edges about what was possible. Many synchronicities happened between the two of us; we were to point the way for each other repeatedly over the next few years.

Steve told me that an energy school offers training in recognizing and applying energy for healing. One would also experience personal healings in that process. He recommended the well-known Barbara Brennan School of Healing, then in New Jersey. Barbara had been a NASA physicist and now was perhaps the leading authority on energetic healing in the country. Her book, *Hands of Light*, was familiar to most of the energy healers and other holistic practitioners I knew.

I had heard of Barbara's school but felt that if I had to travel I preferred being in the Southwest or the West, which I thought would support my own healing.

Coincidentally, just a few hours earlier, Steve had spoken with a mutual acquaintance who told him about another school with a great reputation. This was the program developed by a medical doctor named Robert Jaffe. I took the phone number of the school and, with an excitement I had not experienced for some time, stopped at a country store on a desolate road. With my fingers numbed by the freezing air, which had dropped to thirty degrees below zero not including wind chill, I dialed the outdoor phone knowing this was something I had to do; it couldn't wait. My first question: "Where are you located?" When the person told me they were in Sedona, Arizona, I was so elated I jumped up and down on the icy pavement like a little kid. I had recently taken my first trip to Sedona with Denise and had loved it. I decided, on the spot, that I would enroll, and told the person on the other end of the phone to save me a place in the incoming class.

I knew without any question that this was the next step for me. When synchronicity is at play, the river flows quickly. All one needs to do is pay attention. When I woke up to start this particular day, I had never heard of a healing school; now, six hours later I had committed myself to an experience of it that would change my life. After my first year at the school, I returned to Steve's house with a video and played it for him and some of his friends. He enrolled the following year and quickly became a star student, another tale of reciprocity at work.

At the Dr. Jaffe's School of Energy Mastery, some of the energy clearings we learned were emotional and noisy. We would yell and scream to release blocked or withheld energy. It sounded terrible but in fact was useful and healing. Steve's wife told me, lightheartedly, that when he practiced the work, which he did in his basement, it sounded like he was killing someone. She couldn't understand exactly what he was doing but accepted it with humor and support.

Another instance of synchronicity came out of my relationship with Steve. He had been attending Native American healing ceremonies near his home and told me about them. The ceremonies were conducted by Godfrey Chips, a medicine man who lived on the Lakota Sioux reservation in South Dakota. The Chips family name was well known among medicine men. One of Godfrey Chips' forefathers, I was told, had served as medicine man to the legendary Chief Crazy Horse. Crazy Horse had a reputation for being bulletproof; much of the credit for that was attributed to protection from the Chips medicine.

I was eager to attend these healing ceremonies, but they weren't open to the public. This dismayed me because I hated to be excluded from events I considered significant and also because I intuited that these ceremonies would be meaningful for me in some inexplicable way. One day Steve told me that he was taking Godfrey to purchase a car and invited me to go along. This gave me an opening to meet Godfrey and gain admittance to the ceremonies. Unfortunately, I was running two hours late that Friday morning and it was obvious I was going to miss our scheduled meeting which was to take place at a prearranged exit on the Massachusetts Turnpike. I reluctantly let go of connecting with them and proceeded to the next exit, about ten miles further east, to attend to other business. As I was leaving the turnpike, I heard a horn and turned to see Steve and Godfrey behind me. They were running behind schedule, as well, and had also scrapped their plans. That fortuitous meeting gave me an opportunity to meet Godfrey. After spending the day with him, he invited me to the healing ceremony that night.

After traveling down a remote country road about an hour from where I was staying, I arrived at the barn in which the ceremony would be performed. A friendly man named Andy greeted me at the gate. He was a white man who had lived on the Lakota reservation for many years. When I told him I was from Jacksonville, Florida, he mentioned casually that he had been there to visit a relative.

I don't welcome the possibility of ships passing in the night, so I approached Andy a few minutes later to find out if I might have met his relative, even though it seemed unlikely since Jacksonville is a city of more than a million people. Because his mother lived thirty miles from me, he said, he doubted I would know her. He added that she owned a massage school on the other side of town. Denise had gone to massage school on the west side of town, and I asked him if Mary, who ran the school, could be his mother. "Yes!" He was so elated by this news that he yelled repeatedly to everyone that I knew his mom. Then he ran to get special handmade Lakota blankets for me to bring to her as a gift. This seemed more than coincidence; clearly, the Universe was inviting my attention.

I received several important teachings that night. The first occurred at the sweat lodge, which preceded the main healing. That evening the men and women held separate lodges. I had never participated in a sweat lodge and didn't know what to expect. A co-ed lodge sounded appealing, but this was not the experience I was offered. After we entered the tent one at a time, hot coals were placed in a hole in the center. The ceremony began with each man who held the talking stick speaking while the rest of us listened. As we went around the circle, each of us shared what was most on our minds. My only recollection from that event was the heartfelt lamenting of a young man who had just lost his dog. He lived alone and this animal had been his longtime companion. He was in mourning and asked us to pray for his dog. The depth of their long-time connection touched me. I also realized that as we went into a deeper meditative state, we seemed to enter an altered, spiritual state. Once that happened, the heat from the burning coals ceased to be a problem for me, as I transcended the discomfort of the physical environment. Maybe this is the purpose of the sweat lodge: to allow people the experience of transcending physical reality.

I also saw how easy it was for me to devalue what I give to life, symbolized here by my contribution to the ceremony. Invited guests were asked to bring an offering of a hundred prayer ties. Each prayer tie consisted of a bundle formed by tying together strings, sticks and ribbons in a precise way. I was personally challenged by the act of tying my shoestrings and so silently calculated, with my business school background, that it would take me several hundred years to make the required number of prayer ties! Instead, I resigned from the prayer tie team and gave a hundred dollars toward the ceremony. Because I contributed in a way different from the others, I was left with the gnawing feeling that I didn't really deserve to attend. In other words, I was prayer tie-deficient. When I mentioned this to the hostess, she told me that, to the contrary, they were short on money and long on prayer ties, and assured me that my particular contribution was very much appreciated.

I also became aware of my ability to recognize a manifestation of God or spirit, and the realization I did this in my own unique way. This teaching emerged from the ceremony itself.

Godfrey entered the healing space dressed in his ceremonial garments. We were all gathered in a circle of about a hundred people inside an old barn. Three people then came forward to receive healings. Each began by telling the story of her illness. I knew one of the women, who had multiple sclerosis and walked in public only with the help of a cane. It was cold – the temperature had dropped below zero – and I sat near the children of a well-known movie critic.

After each person spoke, Godfrey went into a prayer or incanta-tion. I don't remember exactly what happened next, as afterwards people described quite different experiences. Some saw grandfather spirits on horses riding through the barn. Many saw Godfrey lifted up in the air and thrown to the ground. There was a simultaneous scream from one group. I experienced a continuous blinking of lights that I believed came from someone turning the barn lights on and off as a prank or joke. The room looked like a thousand activated fireflies, which distracted me from observing the ceremony and irritated me.

When it was over, I mentioned to some of the facilitators that flashing lights during the ceremony had distracted me. I was told there was no artificial light in the barn and what I had observed was a manifestation of spirit. I knew intuitively this was true and, as I heard the explanation, I felt the expansive sensation of gratitude fill my chest. It was a first for me to fully own such a spiritual experience. Afterwards, we joined together in a feast that included buffalo meat. The celebration continued through the night and concluded when the sun rose.

The following morning, I felt none of the debilitating fatigue, at times crippling, that had become my daily companion. I had not gone to sleep before 10 p.m., as usual, the night before, yet, with no sleep, I was excited and on fire the next morning. My fears had abated, my enthusiasm for life was abundant and my spirit had lifted. I was not one of the people designated to be healed and had done nothing specific of which I was aware. I merely prayed that the three people before us be healed. I realized it might be possible for me to heal just by being in a healing environment. I never learned the long-term results of these three healings, which took place a decade ago. I do know that the woman with multiple sclerosis was mobile without using her cane for some time after the healings. When I saw her on the street, I observed she walked with a confidence and bounce that contrasted sharply with the way she had carried herself previously. It had been a remarkable evening, and I was thankful I had followed the instincts that led me there.

Another synchronistic event took place around the time of my mother's death. During her last week I lived at her home, about twenty miles from mine. Several days before she died, a young puppy appeared on her front steps. This was unusual because she lived in a community where it was unlikely to encounter anything that could be considered stray or wandering. Everything was accounted for in that pristine neighborhood.

During that week, I was preoccupied and gave little thought to the puppy. My children were around and often played with the pup, which served as a happy distraction. After the funeral, my friend Brian offered to take the puppy back to his home in Tallahassee; he lived in a rural area and had plenty of yard space. I was about to say yes and thank him. Then it dawned on me that maybe the Universe had gifted me the puppy as some form of substitute companionship for my mother. This pleased Denise, as she had wanted me to take the dog. Because of the pup's red-brownish color, she named her Chili.

Chili turned out to easily satisfy the criteria of man's best friend, at least this man. She sits loyally at my feet as I write. She grew up to be well behaved, sweet and obedient without any help from a fancy obedience school. She has a great sensitivity to her surroundings and, when something is not right in the house, she lets me know. She has been a good and constant companion and, other than her sustenance, seeks only kindness and love. Fourteen years later, she still has some puppy energy and can be seen from time to time throwing her rag doll in the air or racing through the sand dunes. I realize, in retrospect, that I almost missed this wonderful opportunity. The Universe presented me with a puppy just as my mother was leaving, and I recognized the magnificence of this gift only at the last moment.

Several years ago, synchronistic events pointed in a particular direction and also raised some interesting challenges for me. I had decided to spend a week or so in a fresh environment and without charting any specific destination headed north. I drove up Interstate 95 until I approached a junction, at which I needed to commit either to continue north toward the North Carolina coast or turn west toward the mountains. I changed my mind several times in the last mile and then, at the juncture, turned the wheel left and headed west toward the mountains. A couple of hours later I thought about where to stop for the weekend and decided on Asheville, North Carolina. Asheville has a reputation as a spiritual mecca, and I had friends from various healing schools I'd attended who lived there. When I arrived in the downtown area, I found most of the hotels and motels completely booked because of a festival taking place that weekend. I ended up being offered a room at a downtown hotel when it received a cancellation just as I arrived at the reservation counter.

I decided to give John and Penny a call. They were a couple I knew from healing school, although it had been a few years since I had been in contact with John and several more years since I had seen Penny. They were genuinely excited to hear from me and graciously invited me to dinner. In the meantime, I went for a stroll downtown. I had walked only two blocks when I saw right in front of me a store named Finkelstein's. Instinctively, I knew the store had a family connection. Finkelstein had been my family name until my father and his three brothers shortened it to Fink when they were young men. When I walked through the front door of the combination pawnshop, jewelry and gun store, I saw photos of family members on the wall, whom I had never met. When I asked the proprietor the history of the store, he told me the Finkelstein family had run it from the early 1900s until more than twenty-five years ago, when it was sold to the current owners. The new owners retained the family name because of its fine reputation. He told me that Mr. Finkelstein, who was the son or grandson of the original owner, was alive and living in a nearby nursing home. Part of my family migrated north to the Carolinas in the early 1900s, but I didn't know where, and over the years had heard little about them. Within an hour of arriving in Asheville, I had stumbled upon my ancestral connections. I returned to the hotel a little disoriented, thinking about this branch of the family and wondering why I had never known its history.

The mysteries continued to unfold at a rapid pace. Before dinner, John and Penny invited me to hear a speaker, Tanai, from the Institute of Noetic Sciences. She was a former physicist who had been involved with the making of atomic bombs and now was teaching a course on love. This fascinated me. If this woman could transition from bombs to love, then maybe there was hope for a former corporate lawyer. We made a strong connection during her lecture. I asked question after question and felt like I monopolized the conversation with the audience. I introduced myself to Tanai after the meeting and told her I hoped our paths would cross again some day.

Later that night, I walked with Penny in her garden in Black Mountain, just outside Asheville. I had not seen her for years but had always been fond of her. She had a dry sense of humor and minced few words in her often intensely straightforward way. We became friends while staying at the same hotel during our time at the Jaffe School. Penny, John and I had solidified our connection at that time by retelling some of the jokes of Lewis Grizzard, the southern humorist, and had spent many hours laughing uproariously with each other. Penny now talked with me about the fairly recent death of her stepfather, Robert Monroe, founder of the Monroe Institute near Charlottesville, Virginia. Monroe had been one of the early pioneers of out-of-body experiences and many famous people had trained with him. The author Elizabeth Kubler-Ross was a regular guest at the Monroe family dinner table when Penny was growing up. She told me that Elizabeth Kubler-Ross and Barbara Brennan had spent time with Monroe during his last days and had helped with his transition.

The next day I spoke to a friend, Deborah, a terrific healer and instructor in her specialty of esoteric healing. Deborah told me she'd heard that I had met Tanai, one of her best friends, the previous evening. "If you want a change or some inspiration," she told me, "Go see Tanai. She lives in a beautiful place outside of town and maybe you'll want to hang out there for a while."

The next day, I went to see Tanai. It was indeed an inspiring, intense change. Tanai lived atop a mountain near Asheville, in a large house with lots of rooms next door to her business partner, Lucia. The two of them were an interesting, powerful pair. Tanai was an ethereal type who was a conduit for higher energies, and Lucia was a high-spirited earth mother whose teachings kept their joint work grounded. They had developed a powerful, compelling workshop that integrated esoteric concepts and pragmatic approaches to the energy and expression of love. It was Tanai's hope to return to Princeton, where Albert Einstein had taught for many years, to offer these teachings to physics classes. The notion that someone could bridge such a wide gap and bring together people with such opposite inclinations moved me. I think she understood it was merely an illusion that kept the heart and the mind, love and science, so separated. This division was just a projection of the divisions that exist within us.

The people who surrounded Tanai and Lucia were connected through their deep interest in exploring higher consciousness. They all embraced spiritual teachings of these women and were committed to conducting their lives as acts of love. They also were dedicated to impacting the social order by changing consciousness. They called one of their beautiful, ambitious projects "America, Choose Love," which they hoped would have an effect similar to the Hands Across America project.

Tanai invited me to stay in her home to explore these teachings and

131

live among her community. What a turn on my path it would have been to join this group of dedicated, fascinating people, in a beautiful setting at the top of a North Carolina mountain.

I attended one of Tanai's and Lucia's workshops and went to several of their full moon meditations. While I was tempted by the personal potential there, I soon realized I wasn't ready for such a radical change, mostly in lifestyle and probably also in consciousness. I stayed connected with the group for a while and remained inspired by their work, dedication and friendships.

That led to the inevitable question about this road not taken: Did I turn away from it because I was unwilling to disrupt my comfortable life, or because it was just too threatening an unknown – even though it may have been what the Universe was calling me to? Or was it simply what it seemed, an adventure into a lifestyle that stirred my longing to live a heart- and God-centered life?

I will never know. I may have missed a grand opportunity or I may have followed my path precisely. Do I have regrets? No; I'm too prag-matic for that. I also trust that if something is truly meant for me, sooner or later I'll hear that call and respond to it. The Universe isn't stingy with its invitations. If there is any stinginess, I think, it lies in the reluctance of we humans to be the free beings we were born to be. Certainly the events of those 24 hours were no coincidence – taking a fork in the road that brought me to Asheville, coming upon family history of which I knew nothing, having a wonderful encounter with friends I hadn't spoken to in five years, and meeting a teacher who had shifted from making bombs to teaching love and who invited me to live a wild new life. In simply paying attention and following my intuition, two of my new lifetime tools, life was becoming quite amazing.

Chapter Ten

FACING MY FEARS

"You gain strength, courage and confidence by every experience in which you really stop to look fear in the face. You are able to say to yourself, 'I lived through this horror. I can take the next thing that comes along.'"
ELEANOR ROOSEVELT, 'You Learn By Living'

Unbuttoned / Ken Fink

I would soon have an opportunity to work with my fears. I was already dealing with fears around health, dropping out of my profession and my change of living arrangements. But I had not fully dealt with how others perceived my changes and the possibility of public derision of the path I had taken. That was about to present itself in a most unlikely way. In deciding how to work with my fears, I looked to the teachings of some of the spiritual teachers with whom I had come in contact.

I had observed many of these teachers face their fears as a normal part of their lives and practice. Sometimes those fears related to their teachings and sometimes to their daily lives, health or family. I seem to learn the most when the teacher is willing to share his or her personal struggles and process.

Dr. Robert Jaffe, founder of the School of Energy Mastery and one of my most inspiring teachers, said that meeting his fears was an intentional part of his spiritual practice. I had first-hand experience of that practice in the early 90s when I was one of his assistants at a five-day workshop at the Omega Institute. Dr. Jaffe had taken a sudden leave of absence from his school and had moved with his family from Arizona to a sailboat in the Bahamas, leaving behind a large student body and following. The scheduled workshop at Omega marked his return to teaching after more than a year away. There were some who thought he had suffered a breakdown; my own perception was that he had suffered a breakthrough. He had reflected on his life, found that it needed adjustment, and opened to a dramatic change. He had risked a lot for this daring and life-changing adventure.

What made the workshop unique was that the teacher was dealing with his fears as a work in progress in front of his students. This was not merely intellectual exploration; he was confronting his demons in the moment and sharing that process with us. When Dr. Jaffe stood before the class the first day, he began by telling us that this was a painful experience for him. He confessed that he didn't want to be there; he had come in part because he had paid a large deposit to the institute, which he would have to forfeit if he failed to show up. He went on to tell us that this was the most vulnerable point in his life and that he felt fragile. We could all see that, as his feelings were quite visible. He said he didn't know what he would teach us since what he had taught in the past now seemed invalid, and the contents of what he was to teach in the future had not yet emerged. But he also believed, he said, that a group such as the one assembled before him didn't come into being by accident. There was always a common purpose or interest that drew people together. He felt that this group had come together with a common intention, perhaps unconscious, of seeing what the new teaching would be, and to participate in its birth and evolution.

The room was spellbound in the face of a teacher admitting his darkest fears, showing his pain and confusion and speaking his truth. Dr. Jaffe continued in this deeply open and courageous mode, and the days that followed turned out to be one of the most powerful learning experiences I've ever had.

Another inspiration for me of someone facing his fears was when Fred, my friend from college, set out to create his own business. Fred had worked most of his life for large accounting firms within a specialized area. He was a prodigious worker with boundless energy and enthusiasm, but those qualities paled in comparison with his unique ability to deal with people. Fred liked people and had genuine concern for them, and people liked to be with him, in turn.

The last firm Fred had worked for had made certain promises to him that he expected to realize after another year with them. At the end of that year, Fred felt the firm hadn't met its promises and so he considered going into business for himself. Since he was looking at entering a specialty area where a couple of large firms dominated the market, he was fearful of being a small player in a large market.

I met with Fred several times, as one of his advisers, to talk about his reluctance. We tried to uncover the beliefs beneath his fears. This was somewhat of a shift for us, since Fred had advised me more than I had advised him, until then. But something about either the process or the role reversal made me nervous. We had arranged one meeting at a familiar delicatessen in Pacific Palisades, a suburb of Los Angles. Fred was late, which was uncharacteristic of him, and I waited until it was an hour beyond the appointed time of our meeting. Finally I rose to stretch my legs and there, on the other side of a partition not ten feet from where I had been sitting, was Fred, wondering where I was. I felt I wasn't able to sense that he was right there in the same room because I was out of balance from my own apprehension.

Fred's worries focused mostly on his future clients. He worried that if existing clients didn't contact him to continue working with him, he might not generate enough new business to make his new enterprise work. He decided, finally, to look his dragon straight in the eyes and then immediately became clear about what was going on. He realized his focus had been too narrow and was based on all the things that could go wrong. "Instead, I've forgotten to focus on all the new business that could come my way," he told me, "and all the possibilities there are of making this company work. I've overlooked my strengths and my long history of overcoming obstacles to manifesting exactly what I want. I've also forgotten about all the unknown assistance likely to show up once I commit to move forward."

When Fred was able to look directly at his fears and see through them, he was then freed to take the necessary first steps. He developed a thriving practice in a short period of time. New clients came out of the woodwork when they heard he had his own firm, and more work came to him than he could at first handle. In addition, many of the professionals from his prior firms came to work with him. He now operates the practice that he always dreamed of.

Often the external world mimics our internal reality. A chaotic external life may reflect a chaotic internal life, and an obsessively ordered external environment may mirror a rigid internal environment. As the saying goes, "As within, so without." Several years ago I considered life changes that caused me great anxiety. The following incident happened, I believe, as a graphic and vividly symbolic outpicturing of my deepest fears at the time.

I am afraid of snakes, a fear that has persisted since childhood. I don't know why, particularly, other than that I just don't like their creepy, crawly nature. The Bible placed a bum rap on snakes and I guess that held for me, as well. But I know that the snake symbolizes transformation when used as an animal totem, and I understand that transformation is positive. When I'm facing an important shift in my life, I often encounter an actual snake, and that snake often appears on a trail or walkway in front of me, literally blocking my path. Snakes often show up in my dreams, as well, during periods of change.

As I approached my house several years ago, at a time when I was contemplating major changes, I encountered a large snake, about four feet long, in the atrium near my front door. I telephoned a few brave friends with reptilian talents, but no one was available to dispense with it. The local snake busters, who I had called once in the past, had gone out of business. With some embarrassment, I telephoned the animal control division of my city government, but they were out to lunch. I left a message that I really needed their expertise, and soon.

While I waited for help, I stepped outside and took another peek in the hope that the snake had vanished. Instead, I saw the head of a large frog inside the snake's mouth. The snake was in the process of swallowing the frog. While I had found it difficult to watch the snake when it was motionless, it was chilling to watch this hapless amphibian going down the hatch. The frog looked back at me and seemed innocent and calm, I thought. What I found most chilling was its apparent lack of awareness that it was being eaten.

As I continued to watch this drama unfold, my vision blurred and my perception became confused. I thought that I was watching one animal, half-frog-half-snake, the reptilian version of a mermaid, but with none of the attendant fantasies. For a while I could see only the frog and no snake, and then they would both come into focus.

Why was this drama unfolding in the front of my home, I asked myself? It reminded me of the television show Animal Kingdom, which I never liked, even though the graphic violence of nature was safely contained within my TV set. As I recall, the show often depicted the food chain in action. We would look directly into the eyes of a hapless gazelle as it was being devoured by a pack of lions or whatever faster or stronger animal might be preying on it. To make matters worse, the faster and stronger predators often outnumbered the animal being devoured. For some reason, I often watched Animal Kingdom during mealtimes, and equally often felt queasy for the rest of the day. The unstated question for me lurking beneath the drama was: where did I stand on the food chain? Were some unknown bacteria licking their lips, thinking of me as their next meal? By the time animal control arrived, the frog had totally disappeared into the snake. They quickly captured the overfed, misshapen reptile with a pair of long grips and the incident, except for some traumatized neighbors, was over.

I believe there are no accidents, and so this event had to have meaning. But how to interpret it? Was I the frog who would be swallowed by the snake, a metaphor for being swallowed by my fears? If so, would this happen if I were willing to face my fears or, conversely, if I ran from them?

While my micro-analysis led nowhere, I soon became aware that peace had returned to my house within minutes after the snake was removed. With the snake now gone, so too was my fear of the repercussions that might follow the changes I was considering. I realized from the events in the atrium that any upset brought about by these changes would be short-lived, and peace would be restored quickly. My only lingering doubt was an interpretation that I was the frog and wouldn't be able to enjoy the peaceful aftermath. It remained for me to take the risk and see what life brought in its wake – a satisfied snake or digested frog.

A person can attract the very thing he fears by thinking about it too much or obsessing over it. This is a corollary to the belief that it liberates the psyche and life to face one's fears. There is also an energetic principle that holds that whatever we give our attention to expands.

A personal instance of attracting that which I feared occurred around a teaching event. I was at the Inner Focus School of Healing founded by Sandra Parness, a gifted teacher, healer and friend. She had been a senior teacher with Dr. Jaffe's School of Energy Mastery and then established her own healing school in my hometown of Jacksonville. At that time I served as a volunteer on her faculty. I was to demonstrate a section of the teaching about the fifth chakra, which is the expression center governing all forms of communication and is located in the throat. I knew that my friend Jill, an intuitive, teacher, and columnist for a local digest, had made huge posters depicting each of the seven chakras for use in her own teaching. I knew that her fifth chakra poster would aid me immeasurably in my demonstration.

When I went to borrow her diagram, Jill told me that this poster was irreplaceable and asked me to handle it with kid gloves. This admonition activated my fears. I had found that inexplicable calamities befell me in disproportionate frequency with other people's possessions. I had stopped borrowing friends' books since it was embarrassing to return them in mangled or deteriorated condition. And so I obsessed about protecting Jill's poster, although I couldn't imagine what could possibly happen to it.

At the end of the event, which occurred at an oceanfront hotel, I exited the building with poster in hand. I was thrilled that I had successfully concluded my demonstration with the precious object intact. But just as I stepped from the building, a single, powerful gust of wind suddenly blew out from the ocean and snatched the poster from my hands, sending it airborne. I watched helplessly as it continued its ascent and disappeared over the top of the six story hotel. Had it not been for my fear, I believe, the isolated wind gust would probably never have found me. Obsessing on this dread had a direct connection to the very result that I wanted to avoid.

One of my fears was the potential for public derision of my spiritual journey, which had now continued for more than ten years. It was not that anyone was paying particular attention to what I was doing; it was just my fear, then irrational, that my interior process would be trivialized. Little did I know I was facing the possibility of my spiritual journey being made a matter of public record and being judged by a jury of my peers.

The issue that brought this on was a traffic accident, a seemingly insignificant event in the greater scheme of things. But it was to be very important to me, as it would flush out many of my core issues. It was the mid-1990s, and I was in my hometown stopped in expressway traffic when suddenly I was rear-ended. It was a strong jolt and stunned me. I was curious that I did not immediately get out of the car and told myself that this must be what it's like to be in shock. Once I finally moved, I found that I was in an altered state. My car was struck by a young man, probably in his twenties, who had worked a night shift at a nearby chain store and was just returning from work. He was polite and concerned that he had hurt me. I declined an ambulance and decided to proceed with my plans for the day. But about an hour later I started experiencing pain in my neck and back and numbness in my arm, and went immediately to a nearby doctor's office for x-rays and treatment. Over the next few months my symptoms increased and I underwent various treatments, including cortisone injections in my neck and near my spinal column, which were dangerous and painful. A MRI showed that I had disc problems in my lower back and neck.

What had I done to attract a rear-end collision into my life? "Collision" means wake-up call and "rear-ended" means being blindsided, so to speak. From what lethargy did I need to be jolted, I asked myself?

One of the first things I considered was if I had any legal redress, but I was advised to wait at least a year to see if the injuries disappeared or continued. I had asked the insurance company to compensate me only for excess medical expenses and for my physical pain and suffering. When the insurance company met with me, instead of offering a reasonable settlement, which I had expected, they presented me with a surveillance videotape that had been taken of me by their hired private detectives, who had been following me for weeks. I learned that two men had waited in the bushes outside my house and had followed me into the gym, where I regularly walked on the treadmill. They also had followed and videotaped me around my community, sometimes using a hidden camera. When I saw the tape there was nothing that indicated that my injuries were faked or exaggerated. In fact, I told friends, I was distressed that my life on tape looked so boring, and thereafter committed to having more fun. Clearly, they were using the threat of continuing the videotaping to intimidate me and frighten me into a settlement.

I certainly didn't want a public trial of my personal life, but the insurance company wouldn't waiver. There were several other times in my life when I didn't fight and, instead, gave in to maintain the peace. One of these was around my divorce and another around a failed business arrangement. This time I felt I needed to stand up for myself in a more assertive way.

The initial medical reports all supported my allegations. I had received assessments from three attending doctors, each of whom shared the same opinion about the extent of my injuries and appropriate medical treatment. More than a year after the accident, the insurance company sent me to their specialist, an orthopedic surgeon of good reputation, for an independent opinion. He not only corroborated the other three opinions, but also said the injuries were more severe than the conclusions reached in the other reports. The insurance company would, during the course of the trial, fight tooth and nail to keep their own specialist's report from being admitted into evidence. They attempted to persuade him to revisit or change his opinion but were unsuccessful. Now all four medical reports supported my position.

Several weeks before the trial and about two years after the accident, the defendant sent me to another medical expert, whose business consisted almost exclusively of testifying for insurance companies. His examination was unpleasant and seemed staged. It was recorded by a court reporter, a very young gal, naïve, demure and extremely southern. I was given a robe made of paper to cover myself and during the examination it tore away, but she continued typing and averted her eyes at the same time.

The examining doctor clearly had an agenda of what he did and didn't intend to be included by the court reporter. During his examination I would interrupt and inject details about the accident that he didn't want to be of record, such as the severity of the impact and the total demolition of the defendant's car. This encounter was unpleasant and I was shaken afterwards. I had always thought of doctors as healing friends who would support me. This examination was intended, from the outset, to discredit me.

My case was neither sensational nor of any special interest but, from my perspective, the Universe had concocted this scenario to bring my unresolved issues into focus and perhaps conclusion. It brought together two distinct parts of my life: my past legal career and my current commitment to healing and spiritual growth. In the courthouse library there were photographs of various local bar associations, which included pictures of my father and myself at different stages of our careers. While I had never been a courthouse lawyer, a couple of judges, former friends, waived hello to me as I walked down the courthouse hall. Another judge, who I had known from my days on the board of the YMCA, recused himself from my case.

One day, walking to the courthouse, I met one of the few black judges in the circuit. He had been a young associate many years before, in a law firm in which I was his senior. He remembered me, and as we walked together we brought each other up to date about our lives. I told him about my current focus on spiritual growth. He then made a request that touched me. He said that many of his decisions were difficult and weighed on him, and he would appreciate it if I prayed for him. That was a first for me: discovering that my spiritual assistance had more value than my legal advice in the fields of justice that had once been home for me.

In a synchronistic twist of fate, the judge who had been assigned to my case for almost a year was pulled off the case just a couple of days before the trial began. Out of the twenty-plus remaining judges in the circuit, the new judge was the same one who had been assigned years earlier to hear my divorce case, which I had decided not to fight. Was the Universe giving me a second chance to stand up for myself before the same judge? It appeared so.

I had known my attorney since he had started as a younger lawyer in one of the firms for which I worked. He was a hard worker, smart, and a straight shooter, and I felt pleased that he was representing me. I can become quite anxious and needed someone who would be available to me throughout the process. He served me in that way very well.

The day the jury was chosen, it became clear that the opposition intended to place my lifestyle on trial. Their strategy was to appeal to the prejudices of a southern Bible belt jury. The insurance company's attorney, in choosing jurors, began by asking if anyone in the pool of fifty or so possibilities had ever heard of yoga. To my dismay, not one of them even twitched; they responded with blank stares. He then asked if anyone knew anything about natural healing and, again, there was no response. I feared that not only was I not going to be tried by a jury of my peers, but I would be tried by a jury from another planet. Yet, I hoped I was underestimating their ability to find the truth.

The first witness we called was one of the detectives who had followed and videotaped me. If I had allowed the defense to call him as their witness, that fact, alone, would have made it look like they had caught me doing something. In my opinion, they didn't have anything on me. I was just going about my business, grocery shopping, cashing a check, doing routine chores. My activities at that time consisted mainly of complying with the doctor's recommendations: walking the tread-mill or riding my bicycle for rehabilitation.

When the examination began, my lawyer asked the detective if he had seen Mr. Fink do anything more vigorous than what was shown on the tape. His answer was that he had not, and this worked in our favor. The implications in the detective's written report made it seem as though I had been engaged in some contraband activity. It read, and I am paraphrasing, "Subject emerged from his house at 7:15 a.m., opened the trunk of an unidentified car, retrieved an unidentified article and returned to the house alone at 7:17 a.m." Essentially, this meant that Fink got his gym shorts from the trunk of his car. We needed to trans-late this language of suspicion into everyday reality.

I was pleased that my son testified for me, and that Steve, one of my good friends, came to my support, as well. At the deposition, Steve had been in tears telling the opposing attorney what a wonderful person I was. While this fell on deaf ears, mine perked up, and I appre-ciated his open display of friendship. My massage therapist testified at trial that he had given over 20,000 massages and I was the most compliant of all his clients in doing what was necessary to heal from my injuries. I had lost weight to relieve any pressure on my back, and had scrupulously done all of the rehabilitative exercises that had been recommended.

The opposition's case was clearly one of intimidation. They wheeled into the courtroom notes from all the mental health counseling sessions I had ever had, including data related to my divorce, relationships and sex life, ready to disclose those details if allowed. This seemed surreal to me. My car had been stopped on the expressway, I was rear-ended while motionless and now, somehow, my personal life was the issue. The opposition used some of this information to contend that my level of discomfort might be exaggerated.

The investigators had also recovered records of chiropractic massage I had received more than ten years earlier, in another state. At those sessions the chiropractor had presented me with a body map and asked me to shade in all the areas that felt tight or that I wanted worked on. I was compelled at trial to review each of these markings, explaining why each mark was not evidence of a preexisting condition.

We were between court sessions one day when one of the interactions most important to me occurred. A lawyer from the opposition asked me if I would speak personally with him off the record. He asked me how I was willing to submit to this ordeal of having my personal life reviewed in public. He said that he had faced a similar situation and that the pressure was too much for him. I told him that I hadn't always stood up for myself. Sometimes I had chosen compromise or appeasement to not rock the boat, but my gut reaction was to see this one through. I told him that in this situation I didn't think I could be at peace unless I asserted my truth. While talking with him, my training and experience in body reading made me aware that he had a frail body and sunken chest. I understood that it was probably difficult for someone involved in such an adversarial daily routine to have so few physical buffers (broad shoulders, barrel chest, strong jaw) against that continually aggressive energy. I wished I could have asked him to join one of the men's groups I facilitated or in which I had participated. He seemed like he needed a good hug, and the courtroom was not a likely place for him to get it. I thought he would probably continue to function in this aggressive arena until or unless life showed him that something else would be better for his emotional and physical well-being.

My spiritual studies had also taught me that balance was needed in all walks of life, especially for a challenge of this magnitude. Balancing my life had never been easy for me, and I had often found the middle ground by taking a bite out of two extremes. In fact, for many years I would observe the polarities in evidence on the night stand by my bed, where wheatgrass stood side by side with my bottle of Tangueray gin and erotic photos would sit in the same pile with books about God.

I had been advised by my attorney to tell the truth no matter what I was asked when I testified, whether or not it hurt my case, but to say no more than required. The more I said, the more material could be cross-examined or contradicted. So I took the witness stand with the intention to be balanced, truthful and brief, knowing that was how I could be most effective.

In my study of Kabbalistic healing, the "Tree of Life" was used as a paradigm for healing. As an oversimplification, in employing certain healing approaches we would embody the aspect of the tree that was most needed. Since I was now in the grips of the legal system, the branch called Gevurah seemed to be most relevant, since it represents law, order, justice and boundaries. Its counterbalancing branch, Chesed, represents unconditional loving kindness, no boundaries, and spaciousness. My teacher had pointed out that law and order was at its best only when tempered by compassion and loving kindness. Conversely, loving kindness and freedom needed to be tempered with a sound structure and order, or else the loving qualities lacked the container needed to be effective. This profound understanding helped me realize that to be most effective as a witness, I needed to be at peace with the legal system, including the defense attorneys, the judge, the jury, the investigators, the insurance company and the opposing expert witness. In applying the healing power of Geverah/Chesed, I needed to embody both states – boundaries and loving kindness – simultaneously.

I had spent the last number of years in more of a Chesed mode, cultivating openness and relaxing my boundaries in the various healing schools and workshops I attended; that part of the tree would be easier for me to identify with. I felt that my challenge now would be to also respect the legal system and all that it was involved with. As I was being cross examined, I used the internal and external practices I had become skilled in. I held in my awareness both branches of the tree while my action was to be truthful and concise. My testimony went well, and whatever they threw at me, I remained unshaken.

The defense had only a few witnesses. One was the fellow who had rear-ended me, but I felt that his testimony helped more than hurt. The other was the doctor who had been called on in the last few weeks to replace their original independent expert, whose unbiased assessment had been in my favor. This new doctor had the reputation of favoring insurance companies, and was known to be personable, glib and able to win over a jury.

His argument was basically that, although my injuries were real, because of my psychological makeup I had a lower tolerance for pain than others with the same condition; consequently, there was less injury than I believed. The doctor pranced up and down in front of the jury and appeared to make inroads with them. I was afraid that he was close to winning them over when providence intervened. He had placed a model of a skeleton before the jury. As he pointed to various body parts to make his case, suddenly the arms and legs started to fall off. He shrieked in a state of panic and clutched at the body parts before they hit the floor, leaving the impression with the jury that between him and me, he might be the one more prone to exaggeration.

As the trial unfolded, I became aware of my judgments about the legal system. I felt that all the technical rulings were going against me until my lawyer pointed out that we were winning our fair share. This helped me observe the process with less bias and to come to respect the judge's sharp, no-nonsense rulings. On their side, I saw, they had been allowed to keep out the testimony of their original medical expert, whose opinion was beneficial to me, and somehow my evidentiary exhibits were not allowed into the jury room; I particularly wanted the jury to have the photo of the demolished car that had hit me. In my favor, my personal counseling records were kept out as not relevant and the insurance company lawyer was not permitted to object to my list of litigation expenses after he had neglected to do so on the previous day.

My most significant insight came on the day the verdict was rendered. I noticed that instead of parking my car near the courthouse, as I had done on all the previous days, I parked in a remote corner of the parking lot. As I wondered about that, I realized I was providing myself with a way to beat a hasty retreat from the courthouse when I lost the verdict. My rationalization was that I had already achieved the personal victory that I had needed by standing up for myself and meeting all the challenges of that process. What I hadn't allowed for was the possibility of a legal victory. Why would I expect so little for myself, I wondered? Why didn't I feel entitled to the whole enchilada? I was aware that if my belief system didn't allow for a real life victory and my actions reflected that limitation, then it would be difficult energetically and spiritually for a jury to rule in my favor. I immediately moved my car to the parking space closest to the courthouse door. I was choosing to no longer be peripheral to my own life. Instead, I was aligning with the possibility of a complete success – here and everywhere else in my life.

After closing arguments, the jury retired and I went to lunch. Over my sandwich I thought about my entire family history having revolved around the law. My father and my only brother were lawyers, as well as my two daughters and a future son-in-law. My parents had chosen the legal profession for me early in my childhood, and now the legal system was going to judge me. I mused that in theory, if I lived long enough, I might be able to play all the roles in a legal dramatic series. I had already seen the vantage from a lawyer's perspective and had once sat on a jury panel. Now I was a party to the action. What would it be like to also, one day, be judge, bailiff, head juror and expert witness?

While waiting for my check, I picked up a periodical with an in depth astrology section. Astrology is not given serious credence in the United States. I have mentioned it several times here because, when done by an expert, it has been incredibly helpful to me. Astrology is taken much more seriously in Europe and Asia but has been considered valuable to some powerful and well-known people here, as well, including former U.S. presidents. In a recent astrological consultation I had been told that it would be to my benefit for the judgment to be rendered on this particular day, a Friday, rather than extending into the following week. When I read the astrology prediction for the day, the hair stood up on my arms. It reported that in olden times, when warriors went to the arena to fight to the death, if they were victorious they would be required to return to fight another day. It said that modern day warriors were often lawyers and businessmen who fought with briefcases and computers in the courtrooms, which were our contemporary arenas. It was very rare in historic times for a warrior to be given a wooden sword for his extraordinary performance; the gift of the sword meant he was not required to return to the arena to fight another day. It went on to say: "Because of your extraordinary perform-ance, you have been granted your wooden sword."

This remarkable prophecy brought tears to my eyes. Maybe this would be the last time I would ever be required to run the gauntlet. I recalled that earlier that week I had actually dreamed of a wooden sword. I felt exhilarated by this confirmation of what I had sensed from the start, that there was a deep and meaningful purpose to this painful encounter.

I returned to the courthouse to nervously await the verdict. I was particularly anxious that I might be required to pay their attorneys' fees if the judgment was lower than what they had previously offered me. They had two out of town lawyers who, in my exaggerated imagination, had stayed at the Ritz Carlton and dined at fancy steak houses during the trial week, and therefore would submit a bill that could empty my wallet.

The jury foreman finally entered the room and I was jolted from my fantasy. He asked the court bailiff if it would be appropriate for a calculator to be sent into the jury room. That was a good sign and I breathed a sigh of relief. An hour later the jury came back with a judg-ment in my favor. It was a large amount for this type of case in this part of the country. Interestingly, it was within one percentage point of what

I had requested from the insurance company during settlement negotiations. I left the courthouse feeling exuberant. I had met my fears and triumphed over them; I had given myself all the help and support I had needed, both inner and outer; and I had received multiple confirmations from the Universe about my right actions, including the grant of a wooden sword.

Unbuttoned / Ken Fink

Chapter Eleven

CONSCIOUSLY DEVELOPING INTUITION

"The intuitive mind is a sacred gift and the rational mind is a faithful servant. We have created a society that honors the servant and has forgotten the gift."

ALBERT EINSTEIN

Unbuttoned / Ken Fink

*M*y experience with groups dedicated to developing extraordinary or clairvoyant abilities was illuminating and broke new ground in my personal consciousness. For me, learning those skills was like learning to ride a bicycle. The more I practiced and let go of fear, the better I became at it.

It began with an exercise. I sat before a fellow student and used my intention to connect with both him and my higher power. We each asked a question about ourselves on a subject about which the other knew nothing. For example, I might ask him to tell me about my childhood or some aspect of my medical history. If I had been asked that question about a stranger a year before, my reaction, probably unvoiced, would have been, "How should I know? I just met you and we've barely spoken." I would have drawn a blank and felt like I'd received a zero on a test. But I soon found that once I stopped trying to figure out the answers in advance, I could give pretty specific and correct information on subjects I consciously knew nothing about. The answers might not have been perfect, but they were at least in the ballpark, and usually quite accurate.

This is not magic. Intuitive ability is always available to us; we need to clear enough interior space and release the concept that it's impossible in order for it to manifest.

It was a victory for me to engage in these exercises without fear of failure. It also required a certain amount of trust that the guidance would come. I learned to sit with my anxiety and have faith that I wouldn't draw a blank. I would wait patiently for the information to come through. It reminded me of an experience in which I had sat for my law school exam in trusts and estates. I was always well prepared but on that exam, for some reason, I looked at the questions and drew a complete blank. The fear grew as 90 minutes went by and I still had no answers to any of the three questions. The difference between these experiences was that in law school, I believed the answer would come from my conscious memory. I had gathered as much information as possible and trusted that, when the question was asked, I would be able to regurgitate the memorized information and add my own analysis. In contrast, when I was seeking non-intellectual information, I would empty my mind of all possible facts, figures and judgments and open it to the great void rather than to conscious memory for the answers.

When I attended the School of Energy Mastery, we practiced specific drills. One person would stand in front of the room while the rest of us would attempt to see how open or closed each of his or her seven chakras were. The seven chakra centers are the main energy centers of the body; they start at the base of the torso and continue upward to the crown atop the head. Each chakra produces a specific color. The importance of working chakras is that there are certain emotional and physical disorders associated with imbalances in each. A healthy chakra is open, spins clockwise and has a clear color.

We would visually measure the individual's chakras on a scale from zero—completely closed—to 360 degrees— completely open. We did this through the use of our inherent powers of observation and intuition. Dr. Jaffe, who was a medical doctor and a clairvoyant, would then diagnose the subject and tell us what he had observed. Sometimes he brought a patient to class who had a known disease or problem, and we would evaluate the subject using the methods we had learned. The medical diagnosis would confirm whether or not we had intuitively located the specific energy imbalances in the system. If I found that a chakra was closed, immobile or spinning backward, I would use one of the different healing techniques I'd learned to try to correct the energetic pattern.

An emotional release resulted in a number of the healings, and the crying, raging and other ensuing dramatic feelings helped the person's "stuck" energy to move. Some of the techniques included the use of sound, voice, "unwinding," and a specific awareness release technique.

Certain healing methods were brilliant in their simplicity. In unwinding, the healer instructed the client to imagine where he was constricted in his body or emotions and then to move physically in the opposite direction to unlock himself. This had an effect similar to the unwinding of a yo-yo. If you took a tangled yo-yo and attempted to straighten out the string, you usually would create a more complex mess than at the outset. On the other hand, if you allowed the yo-yo to hang freely, the string would unwind by itself in a matter of seconds. I found the results from this simple healing process quite beneficial.

I was recently thinking about people's reluctance to use their intuition when I saw a business magazine article about business executives who had lost their ability to rely on their gut instincts in making innovations in their businesses. This was really on point. We often know more than we think, but have been conditioned not to tune into this deep knowing. When we lose the confidence that comes from trusting our instincts, we lose much of ourselves because we are now forced to depend on other people's information, which may be false, manipulated, or not relevant to our unique selves and situations. We then become dependent on sources outside of ourselves and lose the capacity to use our intuition. We devolve into fish out of water or, more precisely, humanoids who have forgotten to use the compass of our inner knowing— one of our greatest inherent gifts.

Many people engaged in mainstream work rely on their nonlinear knowing in addition to the books and sophisticated technology available to them. A cardiologist friend told me that in almost 95 percent of his cases he was able to determine from the personal physical examination and informed instinct which clients would have major heart problems within the next year. He would use the more sophisticated tests and scans to confirm what he already knew.

Many great athletes report that, in moments of particularly extraordinary performance, they rely on instinct. Most athletes perform within certain predictable parameters. The magic moments, the ones that generate the play of the week, month or year and are replayed for years or decades to come, are typically when the athlete went beyond himself and his level of training and conditioning by tapping into something bigger. In that one brief moment, he was no longer relying solely on his learned Xs and Os. Lance Armstrong's annual assaults on the mountains of France to seize the yellow jersey in the Tour de France are perfect examples; already an incredibly conditioned and mentally tough athlete, he steps it up another notch. Even his chief competitors stumble for words to describe what they just witnessed—at their expense. When we celebrate his success, we are acknowledging the presence of a mysterious factor, one we can't accurately name. The best we can do is say that the athlete was "in the zone."

In Dr. Jaffe's healing program, we experimented in a variety of ways with perceiving information without the use of our ordinary senses of sight, sound, smell and touch. For example, you can feel an energy field when you close your eyes and move the palms of your hands toward each other; at some point before your palms touch, you can feel, but not see, the subtle energy between your hands. Also, if you walk toward someone, you can each feel the other's energy field before you bump into each other. Since the magnitude of people's energy fields varies, you might encounter one person's field at five yards and another's at only three feet.

Here is an energetic exercise I used successfully in buying and selling cars. It can also be employed in a variety of transactions. If you are selling you can use your hands to arrive at the price ceiling, knowing that beyond that point you had exceeded the likely limit. Move your hand up while stating the desired price until you feel resistance. Or, you can lower your hand until you feel it meets support. You have peaked at resistance and bottomed at support. Ask the question, "How much should I ask for my car?" Starting at, perhaps, $10,000 move your hand upward in $500 increments until you feel energetic resistance against it. If you feel resistance at $12,500, you would know that's as far as you can go at this time. You could then check the blue book value for the year and condition of your car to confirm if you're in the ballpark. It is important how you state the question. You might get a different result if you asked, instead, what's a fair price to charge rather than the highest price. You could then use the information from your intuitive response in combination with the facts in reaching your decision.

I noticed that in all walks of life people made decisions based on the energy they felt in a situation rather than on mental analysis, although they would not necessarily be aware of the substantial part their energetic reaction had played. This was usually not conscious. However, in the world in which I was immersed since I became ill, I observed people consciously giving great weight to their energetic reaction to a situation. I once made a pitch to the Jaffe organization about assisting them with their programs and was asked to speak before the governing board. A few minutes after I launched into my sales pitch, I noticed that each of the seven decision makers had their eyes closed. My first thought was that they looked ridiculous. But I knew they weren't asleep. In addition to hearing the specifics of what I was saying they were tuned into the energy of my presentation and its resonance with their purpose. They were assessing if our energies were compatible and if we could work well together. Their determination was "yes" my energy was compatible and I could help; however the organization dissolved before there was an opportunity to implement the decision.

Thus, I was routinely becoming more strongly attracted to the importance of my energetic reactions to situations in my decision-making. I noticed that this was common in many segments of our lives; yet, I also had never before consciously delineated that this was an "energetic reaction" which words previously had felt hokey. In the business world, I would hear decision makers say that the "intangibles" either make or kill a deal. Similarly, in the sports world, intangibles were also considered paramount. I would read in the sports section, before a big game, that one team is rated better than another in most categories—better speed, more strength, a better coach and a home field advantage—but the second team is rated ahead in intangibles. The team with the intangible advantage often carried the day. Afterwards, sportswriters, who are married to statistics and other predictable tendencies of a team or individual, often find it impossible to articulate what the intangible advantage was—probably why that particular catchall word is used.

My newfound interest in energetic reactions broadened my world

Consciously Developing Intuition

considerably. Instead of being excited about a life that may be broader than we had previously thought, in this culture we are prone to suspicion, contempt and fear when the non-rational, non-physical is mentioned or discussed. Forgotten is the likelihood that, in a benevolent Universe, new systems and tools for understanding reality come with evolution and are likely to make this world a better place, individually and collectively. I noticed that as I became more awake to myself, the best guidance I could seek was that of my own inner wisdom. Doing this invited self-trust and confidence. There are many ways to tap into this rich source. For me, a simple one was to ask a question in meditation or prayer and then listen for an answer, which may come immediately or show up in an unexpected way or in a dream in the days that followed.

In asking the Universe to provide guidance, I often go into nature and perhaps connect with a tree, a rock, or a bird with which I feel resonance and then allow myself to be shown what I am seeking. Answers always come to me in nature. The first time I consciously invited the natural world to help me many years ago, I asked if my children would be okay living with my ex-wife, outside of my home. Although they would be in frequent, maybe even daily, contact with me, as we were in the same community, I was at first uncomfortable with this prospect. In seeking guidance, I found myself looking at a large tree and noticed that its branches intertwined with branches of other trees. Some of the large branches protected smaller branches of other trees, while smaller branches of the large tree fell under the protection of nearby trees. From this experience I realized that protection for my children would be there, even it were partially under another branch, while my own protective ability might spread to shelter others in need of protection in addition to my children. I also saw that there was nothing to fear.

As with the tree, my life would provide exactly what was needed.

Chapter Twelve

HEALING MY HERITAGE

"Ho! Mitakuye Oyasin. We are all related."
CHEROKEE INVOCATION

Unbuttoned / Ken Fink

*T*en years into my journey, I reached a point when the fast pace was finally slowing down and there was the possibility of settling into a pattern of steady growth. In contrast to being moved by a succession of unexpected and disruptive events that had catapulted me from one place to another, I welcomed a more stable pace. My health had stabilized, although I still had periods of profound fatigue. Happily, they weren't as disturbing or lengthy as they'd been. It seemed that the lasting impact of this illness would be with me for life, but I hoped to learn to live with it as both the ailment and me had become gentler over those years. The energy of the "type A" personality was long gone and unlikely to return.

I became aware that a number of the teachings I received through my quest had been surrounded by drama and many outlandish events. In an example that may be extreme, in one school, the teacher jumped on top of a student who had quit on life, to make him struggle to get up. The teaching worked to perfection, but the student broke a rib in the process.I began to question if this drama was useful to the lessons I sought to learn. I was aware that my particular personality was probably drawn to the drama to keep me interested in the journey, and so it served a purpose for me in the early years. But it also had consumed a lot of my energy and distracted me from my path. I saw that, for some people, instead of leaning on drama to awaken them, their growth emerged from deep meditation and prayer. Many teachers have pointed to these practices as the most effective and powerful ways to reach enlightenment.

Most people learn lessons and become spiritually aware through the challenges and the ups and downs of daily life –marriages, families and work. My lessons also came through interaction with groups and in structured settings designed for personal growth. Other people learned in different settings. For example, Brian, a long time best friend since the early 70's, was intimately in touch with the natural world and had learned many of his lessons about higher consciousness through his forays into, and communion with, nature. Group settings and interactions would have seemed foreign to him. He had lived on several Florida marshlands, and I would watch my friend, of a hearty Montana background, walk though the tall grass, sometimes at night and then take his canoe out into the swamp, with lightning streaking in the sky above. When he visited the ocean, he had a unique style of progressing along the shoreline by walking at forty-five degree angles into the water up to his waist, then walking out to the shore, and progressing yet, through these forty-five degree forays.

My most recent spiritual teacher, Jason Shulman, downplayed the dramatic and his own personality in his teaching. Jason had created a school, A Society of Souls, based in New Jersey, for teaching what he has named Advanced Integrated Kabbalistic Healing. As a student of the school, I came to see that he regarded drama as a distraction from the deeper teachings.

I had previously been involved with groups in which miracles were talked about routinely and non-physical entities pointed out and named routinely. Jason did this only on rare occasions and only when noting certain presences were in the service of his teaching.

I hesitate to write about Jason's teaching for several reasons. One is that I cannot do justice to the profundity of what he offers to his students. Each piece builds upon another piece, and some of the groundwork takes years to develop. Secondly, Jason has so many levels of understanding about healing and higher consciousness, and I feel I grasped only a small part in the four years I was with him. Also, I can't replicate the precision and nuance of the way he uses spiritual language. However, I have tremendous respect for the work he does, so with the intent and hope that my personal experiences might help to bring this magnificent work into the world, I will describe them.

During the four five-day weekends we met together each year, we would listen to Jason's lectures, watch demonstrations of Kabbalistic healing work, and then began to practice healings. We were taught to develop a diagnosis that was attained through deep relationship with the other person. We approached the healing with the understanding that it benefited the healer as well as the person being healed. One way to avoid creating separation between the two parties was the use of the terms "vertical Holy One" and "horizontal Holy One" in place of the usual "healer" and "patient," or "client."

Jason set the groundwork by talking about the subject matter in abstractions and then offering concrete examples. He usually demonstrated a healing technique on a volunteer student, and later we practiced with each other under the supervision of his able staff, often people already enjoying active healing practices.

A piece of the training I found particularly useful involved the practice of sitting with our own anxiety while we held a strong interior connection to the person designated for the healing. We were instructed to explore not feeling compelled to cure or to rush to a diagnostic conclusion. It was important, we were told, to become accustomed to being present to our own anxieties and not be driven by them.

In almost all the schools that I had attended, from high school to law school to healing schools, I found that the depth and breadth of the teacher usually impacted me as much as the subject that was being taught. As an undergraduate in business school, for example, I took several courses in Russian history. I, like many others in my class, was drawn by the flamboyance and brilliance of the teacher and the joy in the classroom. Jason is one of those extraordinary teachers. I often felt I was sitting in the presence of history in the making. To me, his work linking the Kabbalah and healing was comparable to Einstein's break-through connections in physics. I also found his personal struggle very human and poignant as he brought himself and us closer to God.

While his teaching of healing was developed out of his study and understanding of the Kabbalah, often called the Books of Jewish Mysticism, Jason brought many other disciplines to his teachings. From his study of psychology he could easily talk about defense mechanisms and personality disorders. He often told stories of Buddhist masters, rabbinical scholars of the Talmud, and Indian yogi-saints to make his point. He also had a rich background in music as a singer and song-writer. Many years earlier, he was in a rock and roll band; more recently, he wrote, sang and recorded songs to God. When he once recited a poem to us, a student asked if it was by the mystic Persian poet Rumi. "No," he said. "It is my own." He had also recently started painting. My work with Jason preceded the love affair between Hollywood and the Kabbalah, as to which I have no judgment. In all events Jason's work was unique and differed from what I would read about in the newspapers.

The scope of the teachings paralleled the scope of the teacher.

Jason's knowledge of the arts, physical sciences, and mathematics enriched his teachings. He sometimes spent a weekend on his computer in search of a rare Kabbalistic text, connecting with scholars throughout the world. Although he had the talent to perform in almost any area at an incredibly sophisticated level, he chose to dedicate his life to healing, the teaching of healers, and helping his students deepen their relationships to God. Most of the students felt privileged to be a part of A Society of Souls and its founder, a rare gift to humankind.

Jason's classes were always infused with a great deal of humor. When in a particular mood, he reminded me of Billy Crystal in the way he would keep the class laughing. He delighted us with his stories and asides in the tradition of the great Jewish humorists. He also had an irritable edge, which reminded me of myself. When there was material he wanted to present, he would quickly become annoyed by distracting noises or inappropriate questions. But I also observed him working to hold his irritation in check. A friend who had known him for many years described him to me as a frustrated angel.

Once I interrupted Jason's solemn rendition of a story with a humorous interlude. The class was in a deeply open and engaged state while he quoted a Chinese sage by repeating a phrase in Chinese three times. With eyes still closed, clearly moved by the story he was recounting, he asked if anybody knew the English translation. Without thinking, and at great peril of an inappropriate response because of the solemnity of the moment, I blurted out, "Location, location, location." Fortunately, it was well received by Jason and the class.

Since my religious background was in Judaism, I felt Jason's school presented an opportunity to reconnect, or at least make peace, with the faith of my lineage. As a kid, I had been active in religious school activities and had served as president of my confirmation class and the religious school student body. But somewhere along the way, I had lost my resonance and connection to the Jewish teachings. I attended religious services only once at college, but when I heard the rabbi speak with a speech defect that sounded like Bugs Bunny, I couldn't hold in my laughter and fled from the room. As an adult, I felt that some synagogues, like some churches, seemed more interested in membership and building drives than in the substance of the teachings. This was a practical necessity, I understood of course, but sometimes the original message for which I attended seemed smothered by the practicalities.

The larger problem for me in any organized religion was that I was repelled by a tendency to motivate people through guilt and fear. Whenever the teaching was exclusionary or manipulative, I felt even more alienated. I felt certain that God or any higher power would not threaten separation or wish to induce fear or guilt. In contrast, when what was spoken was unifying, included all people and was respectful of all paths, I could open to it. This was my litmus test, a simple barometer that has served me well, was the message given unifying or was it divisive?

I have since come to see that organized religion has also done tremendous good. I recently went to a High Holiday service at a nearby synagogue in its incipient stages. We were welcomed from the pulpit at the outset, and it was clearly communicated that no one would ever be excluded from services because of money, membership or religion. I was touched and immediately attracted to the rabbi and congregation. On other occasions, I have seen that it's the humility and depth of the religious or spiritual leader which determines how I relate to their offerings. Over time, I have become less judgmental; I see that God's work comes to us from many sources, religions and beliefs, and through people wearing many different cloths, clothes and robes.

Before applying to Jason's school, I had a healing experience with a renowned homeopathic doctor from Flagstaff, Arizona, who reignited my interest in my Jewish origins. I was looking for a remedy, expertly prescribed, that would make all my problems, physical and otherwise, disappear. After driving up the famous Oak Creek Canyon, a storm fast approaching me as I whipped through the scenic hairpin turns, I knocked on the door of a man named Vega Rosenberg. Because of his name and reputation, I was expecting an eighty-year-old sage. Imagine my shock when a young man, perhaps in his early thirties, yelled for me to come in.

Sitting at his desk when I entered, he announced without any further introduction that he thought he must be a man of great light. When I asked what he meant, he said he had recently taught in England, and just moments ago had opened a letter from a student calling him a Nazi. He explained that great light always follows great darkness. He continued that this was the worst possible thing that could be said to him, especially since he had grown up in Israel. He told me that the last time he taught in England, they merely called him incompetent. "Since they're now calling me a Nazi; it must mean that I am bringing greater light into my teaching," he said.

I had not expected to speak to a homeopathic doctor on religious matters, the furthest thing from my conscious agenda at the time. Vega began by asking me many questions – about my health, emotional issues, background and various preferences. When asked about my religion, I told him that I'd been brought up Jewish but I had found too much manipulation and guilt in organized religion to be attracted to it at this time, whereupon he instantly stopped his questioning and took my hand in his. When he spoke to me, I felt a stillness and penetration that went deeply into my being. He told me that he was raised in organized religion in Israel, and that he hadn't experienced any manipulation or guilt. He explained that Judaism was originally pure, as was true with other religions, but that its practice had been distorted at times (as in all religions) by people and organizations with quite different objectives. "I want to show you something," he said, asking me to close my eyes. He then sang for a long while in Hebrew. Tears flowed down my cheeks and I felt an immediate connection with the teachings and lineage as they must have existed at one time. My energy flowed strongly and my body felt thoroughly alive. I knew I had received a healing far beyond what the homeopathic remedies might do for me.

The majesty of the force of nature that night was in resonance with the importance of this experience. (I tend to connect powerful events occurring together as having some significance, even if I can't explain it.) I headed back down Oak Creek Canyon in the midst of a severe storm. I felt as if my life was in danger; it was. Only one other car was on the road and we followed each other's taillights in a protective game of leapfrog; we had some sort of unspoken agreement to help each other through the storm. On the hairpin turns, with their potentially fatal drops into the abyss below, I could barely hold my car steady against the high, howling winds. I felt deeply thankful when I finally arrived safely at my motel. I learned the next day that flash floods had erupted in the canyon shortly after I'd returned and that people had been washed away and killed.

One motive I had in applying to Jason's school was to heal my rift from Judaism. I quickly learned I had not merely chosen a tremendous teacher but a great subject, as well: the Kabbalah. But it felt strange to be applying to a school in my fifties, although that may have been the median age of the other applicants. Most students were established in their careers, highly educated and very grounded in their lives. By all indications, this was an advanced program. I learned that in historic times one was allowed to study the Kabbalah only after he was forty years old, married and well established in the community. Our school was not about a didactic study of the Kabbalistic texts but, instead, used the Kabbalah as the basis for the unique system of healing developed by Jason.

The admission process reminded me of applying to Ivy League colleges in the '60s. There were around 200 applications per class and each class was limited to forty people, so only about one in five applicants was accepted. Another aspect of the process, which I appreciated, was the telephone interview personally conducted by Jason. I believe he narrowed down the original group of applicants and then called each to discuss why that person wanted to be in the school and to answer any remaining questions. Demonstrating this degree of care – the brilliant head of a school taking time to speak to each applicant personally – was profound for me. I sensed that Jason joined an attunement to divine intelligence with his linear mental intelligence in making his admission decisions. During the course of the interview, I also was in attunement with the divine to discover if and how I would resonate with Jason's teaching.

I was also attracted to the name A Society of Souls. I had been with other groups because we liked to vacation or exercise at the same place or cheered for a team that wore the same colors. It would be a beautiful experience for me to be part of a group selected because of our soul qualities.

I immediately felt a kinship with the people in the class. These were spiritual seekers with high intelligence, deep hearts, and many types of prior studies under their belts. There was a common intention to make this work for all of us. Most people in the class were engaged in some type of healing practice. They included psychologists, mental health counselors, healers, massage therapists, medical doctors, midwives and chiropractors. Several classmates were from other countries including Canada, Italy and the Netherlands.

I had often thought about how I might ultimately be of service, but knew it was unlikely I would start a healing practice. Would taking this training be a waste of a valuable and limited slot? I refused to linger in these habitual thoughts that denied my potential contribution. I trusted Jason's intelligence and that of the Universe. I believed I might someday touch some human being in some unknown way because of my studies, and that might contribute in some way to the transformation of the world. I might come to know about such an event, or it might forever remain unknown to me.

This teaching provided an important grounding to my spiritual experiences. Jason did not glorify or even give much attention in class to his clairvoyance, or anything else that might separate him from his students and teaching assistants. At first, I missed the drama. I had become addicted to it. I told my friends and whoever else was willing to listen my stories of the extraordinary events. I believed this drama might justify my detour from a more predictable or mainstream path. But in A Society of Souls, extraordinary moments often passed in silence. We all basked in the depth of the experience but had no need to dramatize it.

Jason taught us about the different spiritual Universes described in the Kabbalah. Some of these were accessible to us in human form, while others were only partially accessible or not accessible at all. During our final year, he taught us about Briah, a Universe very close to God and accessible only under certain conditions by humans. As he spoke of this dimension, he became so moved that he could barely speak; tears filled his eyes. He appeared to be looking into the kingdom of heaven. I was able to ride his experience, which in itself was wonderful, since I was unable to access this realm on my own. Through these various teachings I became more grounded both in myself as a person, in my skills to help other people, and I came to have faith in the divine plan and where I fit in, although I could not recite the details. The trust that evolved came from a place other than mental analysis, and carried the message that "all is well."

My favorite story of Jason's came when he told us to consider a period of time when we were no longer alive, and everyone who we have ever known was no longer alive, and there was no memory of anybody who had ever known us or who we had known. He said that if today we were able to love ourselves just a little bit more today, it would create a light that would go forth into the Universe. At this later period of time, when we had ceased to exist and memories of ourselves and all we'd known had ceased to exist, the light we created today would still be alive and available in the Universe.

Unbuttoned / Ken Fink

Chapter Thirteen

THE UNIVERSE PROVIDES
SECOND CHANCES

"I'm astounded by people who want to 'know' the Universe
when it's hard enough to find your way around Chinatown."
WOODY ALLEN

Unbuttoned / Ken Fink

The Universe often gives us a second chance, particularly with experiences that originally seemed to turn out badly or unfairly. While these second chances are not automatic, they sometimes show up as benevolent self-correcting mechanisms. The correction might be obvious, or it might be obscure or not happen at all. At our current level of knowing, I don't think we can be certain about what is unfair or needs to be changed—only to be open to the change when it presents itself.

During the period following my illness, I became aware of receiving a second chance in several situations in which I felt life hadn't treated me fairly. When such a correction has happened to me, it seems to follow my having made an internal correction, which subsequently is mirrored externally. I had an agreement with a friend Bill whom I had originally met in Philadelphia at the end of my college days to share a fee based upon my referral. He had offered sixty percent to me, but I told him I would rather divide our profit fifty-fifty so we would be equal partners. When he received the first part of the fee, he honored the agreement and paid me. But when the second installment arrived, he kept most of it and gave me only a token percentage. When I protested, he said he had spent the money. This hurt me, not only because I needed the money but also because he was a close friend; I felt baffled by his betrayal. He said he had to put in more work than expected, that the transaction took more than a year longer than expected and that I had not been a great help. But we had made a handshake agreement on the fifty-fifty split and he had mentioned nothing about his change of heart nor asked for my greater participation in the present until the time came to divide the check.

I wrestled with the issues around this for several years. I thought that maybe my newly adopted casualness made me an easy target in a business deal; I had been lax in not documenting our agreement in writing. I also realized my shadow had been projected onto him, that part of me which considered taking advantage of someone else, even though I tended to overcompensate for my dark side by giving up more than my share.

As soon as I made peace with what had happened and stopped replaying the "unfair" scenario, I unexpectedly received a windfall from another source in exactly the amount I had been under-compensated. I was stunned that the Universe had taken away with one hand but given back with the other. I had fantasized my friend would ultimately see the error of his ways, come to me with profuse apologies and make good on the difference, allowing our friendship to be restored. But the compensation, instead of coming directly from the person who owed it, came to me through a third source. It took awhile for me to connect the two events instead of dismissing the sequence as a coincidence, but I fully believe that this was how the Universe made the correction.

I have since forgiven my friend and spoken to him several times. I don't have any remaining feelings about the subject, so I know I have healed that hurt. I also remembered that in the past, he was the first to step forward and support me when I was at my lowest point; he extended his hand several times. I decided not to judge him solely on my interpretation of our last encounter and to be open to his story, which might sound quite different now that my charge about it was gone.

Another second chance involved the law firm in which I had been a partner at the time of my illness. The firm was formed when my original firm restructured. I'd worked for the prior firm for eleven years when most of the corporate department left to join a smaller group with whom we'd had a positive history. At the time we made the shift, we were a hot commodity, partly because we were good lawyers and partly because several large institutional clients were coming with us. We all met one morning in the kitchen of one of the partners and outlined our new partnership understandings on the back of a napkin. I didn't question that process, as this was an exceptional group of lawyers with an honesty, directness and clarity of purpose I trusted. They were terrific, good-humored people and, in contrast to my previous firm, nobody tried to climb the ladder over another's back.

I felt privileged to be a part of this organization. I had practiced with this firm for a little more than four years and felt I was entitled to retirement or sickness benefits upon leaving since I believed the eleven prior years counted, as well. My partners granted me a leave of absence when I became sick and reserved an office for my return. Since we had never signed an official partnership agreement, however, they took the position that no long-term benefits would be paid. I felt we had always had an understanding to the contrary and I was acutely disappointed. I also knew that this position might be setting a guideline to which others in that original group would themselves be subject one day. However, I had no choice under this interpretation.

About a year later, my doorbell rang. I received an unexpected courier package with a revised partnership agreement and a note requesting that all partners sign it. The firm needed to furnish the new agreement to the bank by the end of the day in order to finalize a line of credit. Apparently the firm had forgotten they were treating me as a partner for some purposes, but not others. I signed the agreement and returned it as requested. After another year, when I was still on a leave of absence and unable to return to work, I resigned my position and asked for my benefits under the partnership agreement. I really don't know the extent of the deliberations on the other side. I understand that there were many meetings and a couple of factions in disagreement. We spoke through our attorneys for about a year, but the firm resisted paying me. Finally, when they were ready to reach a settlement, I agreed to about seventy percent of what had been due me.

After feeling for a long time that I had been treated unfairly, I came to realize I hadn't considered myself deserving of these benefits. I had told myself I had an illness with no real name and which, on some days, didn't even seem real. Also, not working went counter to my family's belief system; no one had ever worked harder than my father, and I was raised to believe men were born so they could get up and go to work every day. If I didn't do conventional work, I wasn't legitimate. Today, I can see that I needed those couple of years to get to the point where I felt deserving of the benefits due me. Once I did, the Universe provided me with what was originally contested.

Another situation in which the Universe gave me a second look involved the birth of my first grandchild, Lillie. Her mother Allison, my daughter, had been born at a time when my life was very busy. It was late September 1971, and I had just started my first permanent job. The competition for a place with a good law firm had been keen, as most of my job-seeking peers had been in the top ten percent of their classes and from the best law schools. I was due to take the bar exam on a Monday morning in Miami, about 400 miles from where I lived. One of the senior partners had visited my office before the bar exam and reminded me with an off-hand laugh that we were the oldest continuous law firm in the state and that no lawyer in the firm had ever failed the bar exam. If this was meant to put me at ease, its effect was just the opposite. Would I have the dubious distinction of being the first attorney to fail? My anxiety ran wild. I had planned a full day's review the day before the bar exam. However, my wife went into labor at midnight on Saturday, so I found myself in the hospital labor room, just hours before the last flight to Miami. When my wife dozed off between contractions, I stole furtive peeks at my notes. We discussed whether I should leave to take the exam or see the birth process to conclusion, in which event I would apply to retake the exam in four months. We decided that I should take the exam the next day. The doctor, unknown to us, gave her something to speed up her labor, and Allison was born on Sunday morning, September 26, 1971, a few hours before my flight departed.

By the time I reached Miami for the two-day exam, I was exhausted; I had been up for the previous forty-eight hours. When I spoke with my wife after I finished the test, I learned everything was not okay. For a few hours there was concern about whether there might be any health issues about Allison, which were quickly dissipated by a call that it was a false alarm. She turned out to be brilliant and beautiful, but we didn't know this at the time. I decided not to stay and celebrate after the exam, which I passed. I rented a car and drove all night, as fast as I could, to get to the hospital.

When I arrived, my mother and father-in-law were in the room. Allison had not yet received a middle name, and they wouldn't allow her out of the hospital until the birth certificate had been completed. While Allison happily turned out to be a healthy baby and an extraordinary person, her birth didn't go smoothly for me, in part, because I was also focused on other pressing matters at the time and being out of the city, I felt pulled in two directions at once.

Twenty-eight years later, Allison was ready to give birth to Lillie. I was aware that twenty-eight years completes the astrological cycle of Saturn, a major shift point in anyone's life; it's a powerful time for releasing what's transpired and setting a new pattern for what's to come. I also realized I had separated from Allison's mother after fourteen years, the exact mid-point of that cycle and thus a time of major readjustment, so I might be revisiting some old issues there. When I consulted an astrologer, he told me that, although Lillie was not due for several weeks, she would probably be born an "air sign" which meant no later than June 22, before the sun moved out of Gemini. That was three weeks early. I passed along my prediction of Lillie's birth date to Allison's husband, Scott, an obstetrician and gynecologist, who teased me about it. When Allison went into labor on June 21, my second-hand prediction was given credibility and I immediately retired from the prognostication game.

Interestingly, a number of the same people who were present at Allison's birth were also at Lillie's birth. I decided that I wanted to be there this time with full, undivided, undistracted attention, quite unlike the scene twenty-eight years earlier. Scott delivered his own child, the birth went smoothly and it was beautiful. My ex-wife's husband, a practicing lawyer, was tied up at work and couldn't come until the next day. The maternal grandfather had trouble with his evening flight, and weather problems the next morning, which gave me the unusual opportunity to be present with my children. So that night, after the birth, I took my ex-wife, our two other children, and her son from her second marriage to dinner. I sat at the head of the table of what had formerly been a family. For me, it was a moment of peace, grace and celebration, a momentary reconstitution of what had been. I felt the cooperation of the Universe in this wonderful revisiting of a critical moment in my life, the birth of a child into my family.

Both Lillie and Allison have an unmistakable family resemblance. I once sent Allison a photograph of my father from 1913, when he was three years old and still had long hair. Her housekeeper saw the picture and asked Allison why someone had dressed Lillie up in those old clothes, confusing Lillie with her great-grandfather. It also delights me that Allison attended both the college and the law school I had attended and, in the family tradition, did incredibly well academically. While Allison and I had not been as close during her growing up years, as I would have wished, the birth of her children, my grandchildren, created objects of mutual love, which provides an opportunity for me to be closer to my daughter Allison, which has been my long time desire. She is clearly a blessing in my life which manifested after years of what seemed to be a disconnect.

When I think of Lillie's birth and how healing it was for me, I recall a similarly deeply healing experience of birth the Jaffe healing school at which I had studied. One of the session topics had been birth, and a pregnant teacher agreed to deliver in front of the 140 students if the timing worked out. This became what had to be one of the most beautiful and supported births of all time. Starting several days before the delivery, people with extrasensory skills came before the class and made predictions about the child and the likely course of her life. The mother went through labor in a private room, with two doctors from the class in attendance, and then came back to our meeting room for the delivery. We all gathered with candles around the altar and chanted, sang or prayed, all this guided by the expectant mother. The birth went like clockwork. A beautiful baby girl was born with the extraordinary support of 140 people.

Afterwards, we all exchanged stories of births we had experienced, including our own. Surprisingly, many of these birth experiences had been very painful; they included forced forceps deliveries, the depersonalization of hospital births, the exclusion of fathers, lack of support for the delivering mothers, and partners not showing up for the delivery at all. Through the teacher's great act of generosity, we saw what was possible when a birth setting includes love, prayer, support and connection with the world of spirit.

In another second chance situation, I observed what happened with a friend who needed to obtain a green card. He hadn't returned to his home of origin for many years and his legal right to remain in the United States was uncertain. There were aspects of the application process that required groundwork for which he hadn't been prepared or willing to address. I don't know the details, but it took him years to take care of the specifics necessary for his application. Finally, after much work and with the help of his attorney, he received the required affidavits and recommendations. He was within a couple of days of actually filing the application, after years of arduous preparation, when he learned that he had won a green card in the lottery held periodically for that purpose. Once he had done the necessary work, the Universe removed the obstacle in his way.

We sometimes hear of people having potentially fatal diseases who, after they deal with certain inner conflict, learn that their tumor has disappeared or that tests show the original problem is gone. Once balance is restored an illness may, indeed, disappear. I know more than one person who has experienced this.

We often also observe this phenomenon in sports. Let's say a player has been kicked off a team, abused, treated poorly or told to go elsewhere. When he returns to his former home stadium and has another chance to prove his skill and value in a way he was unable to do originally, I don't want to bet against his team. In 2001, Trent Dilfer, who had been booed for years as the quarterback of the Tampa Bay Buccaneers, returned to face the crowd, which nearly hooted him off the field a year earlier. This time, he led the Baltimore Ravens to the Super Bowl title as their quarterback. Ironically, Tampa Bay had cut Dilfer because team officials concluded they would never win a Super Bowl with him at quarterback. I assume something woke up in him that allowed this dramatic turnaround to transpire.

While my personal examples of second chances have come with respect to business opportunities or family matters as detailed above, I've observed second chances, as well, with creative people who have completed a book, a song, or a screenplay that, for years, went unpublished or unproduced. Stories like this are often told during acceptance speeches on Oscar night or at book award ceremonies. I believe that in some of these instances of deferred recognition, the artists are not getting the credit they deserve because something is out of balance in their own psyches. They may believe that they're not entitled to the reward, or that their work isn't as good as another's, or that they are otherwise undeserving. They may believe the work is imperfect, incomplete, or not legitimate in some respect. Or, they may feel they have stolen the concept on which the work is based. The Universe then complies with their own evaluation by deferring acceptance or recognition of their work. The outer "failure" can be corrected when the person corrects the imbalance internally. He might realize, for example, that no creative act will ever reach perfection, and that he has nevertheless made a valuable contribution; he may now feel that he deserves accolades because he, himself, had exaggerated the flaw way beyond its relevance. When I see a play or other work of art go public after a period of deferred recognition, I know that on some level some internal change has allowed for the outer success. Because of my experiences and observations, I find that when I am not receiving the external recognition I feel I deserve, I look inwardly to see whether an imbalance or feeling of lack of deservingness has caused the external stagnation.

Chapter Fourteen

STRIPPING AWAY THE EXTREMES

"When the solution is simple, God is answering."
ALBERT EINSTEIN

Unbuttoned / Ken Fink

When we're born, life is simple. When it's time to die, life is again simple. Between those bookends we typically become very busy and life becomes complex. We each see life through our own lens, and our unique perspectives are based on the shape and size of that lens, which also is the source of our distortions. Thus, we see what we expect to see and hear what we expect to hear.

One of the many ways to get close to God is to simplify our lives. Things that seem the Godliest are often the simplest. Consider the magnificence of God's gift to us in the form of our family, friend, home, pets, the birds, the trees, the ocean and the stars. While these things seem pretty basic, they are also profound.

As I write, my wonderful dog, Chili, sits at my feet. Chili has been an amazing gift; certainly, she's this man's best friend, loyal, appreciative and cheerful. However, I notice that the more complex my life gets, the less I notice her. We might be in the same room for hours, but the more matters that are on my plate, the less I see my dog. As fathers, we sometimes miss the brief time given us to be with our young children. The smaller they are, the more intention it takes to be present with a child. They can't grab your arm and say, "Listen to me!" Unfortunately because of the pressures of work during my children's youth and the priorities of that day, I missed some opportunities with them as young children I wish I could have back, but because of this awareness have tried to capture important moments as they grew older.

I talk about spirituality a lot; at its core, it could be defined as living in attunement with the flow of life. To be in attunement is to be present, but presence can only happen by being here, now. Spiritual teachers often exhort us to be human beings, rather than human doings. But I notice that many spiritual seekers are just as busy running from one experience to another as they were in the material world. We are each susceptible to fall into the trap of overactivity.

I write about being present because this has been a demanding challenge for me. People are most comfortable when their lives include specific levels of activity. We'll often complain that we're too busy, yet we'll create a new project to get ourselves back to our former level of busyness as soon as a slack period shows up. Once that level of activity is reached, the same level of non-presence is reached. One reason, I think, for the discomfort of reduced engagement is that we often feel less worthy when we're not being productive. When we take vacations, we often make sure that we're always available by mobile phone, pager or fax. I know I fight with feelings of personal identity, who am I and what am I worth apart from what I am producing now and what am I going to do next.

Our western lifestyle of constant activity is one reason, I believe, that spiritual teachers have gained popularity in recent years. They have the potential to keep us busy and present at the same time. Whether it's yoga, tai chi, meditation or any of the martial arts, we need a certain level of presence to be able to do those practices. Like a trapeze artist or high wire performer, we can only be in one place at one time. The constant level of activity I experienced in my former law practice helped create a lack of presence in the rest of my life. When I sat at my office desk, it felt as if I were in the trenches. Every few minutes the phone rang and I would think "incoming" as someone lobbed another question, request or piece of work my way. Part of the problem was my own makeup. Once my mind started to grapple with a problem, I was unable to set aside my thinking about it.

I learned a great deal about personal presence from workshops I attended. I went to the first of these at the request of my wife, who turned out to hate the experience while it opened up a whole new area of inquiry for me. It took place over ten days at the renowned Esalen Institute at Big Sur, California.

Esalen also had been recommended to us by Joseph, a life-long friend from college. At that time, he held a prominent position with Chase Manhattan Bank in London. From our first meeting during my freshman year, Joseph made a lasting impression on me. In that initial meeting at the freshman dorm, Joseph talked about getting the most out of his undergraduate experience while the rest of us were looking for the usual freshmen boy distractions. Joseph held several jobs while in college, including headwaiter of the freshman commons and a night job driving a bulldozer to clear snow from the runway of the Philadelphia airport. He eventually made a huge name for himself in the international financial community and continued to raise his level of consciousness at the same time, a rare combination of achievements. When Joseph recommended Esalen, I was not particularly keen on the idea but, as it turned out, there was something for me in the simplicity of the experience that I found attractive. This was to be a beginning of my unbuttoning.

One aspect of simplicity introduced to me at Esalen was an understanding of how I approach life. The group leader, Janet Zuckerman, who became a legendary teacher at Esalen, asked me to remove my glasses for the week; I complied. I noticed over time that I could see much better than I thought possible without them. That was the point. I had become so dependent on my glasses – along with all the other devices in my life – that I'd forgotten I had some ability to get along without them.

Next, Janet instructed me to walk around for two days with my head jutted forward in an exaggerated fashion. I looked like a large ostrich with head pointed forward (instead of in the sand), but unable to see important parts of my surroundings. She told me this was how I approached life, by leading with my head. She wanted me to embody that trait and exaggerate it so that I would kinesthetically get how it affects me. It was a strange request, but I agreed. I realized that while other people might lead with their hearts, emotions or physical bodies, lawyers usually lead with their heads. This is how we are trained. Being head people, we are also verbal and competitive, so we can usually out-duel other people with words including those with whom we are in intimate relationships.

We spent one day of the workshop dealing with our feet. I had not thought about my feet in years; somehow, they never entered into my hundreds of musings about the complexities of the corporate law. I had even considered it a nuisance to buy a new pair of shoes. We talked in the workshop about how we had been connecting with the earth, and we then walked barefoot through the grass and dirt to savor that connection. We massaged each other's feet and were shown accupressure points that activated different organs and body systems. It was strange spending a day focused on my feet, yet they are the bases of the structure that supports our bodies. We would get along poorly without them. Now and then, I recall this teaching and remind myself to take off my shoes and glasses and walk on the grass or beach.

The Esalen experience also taught me about being present in my body, which was particularly difficult for me and remains so today. We were reminded that the body is the temple in which we live. It helped to remember what the New York Yankee slugger Mickey Mantle had once said, "If I knew I would live so long, I would have taken better care of myself."

We also talked about sensuality and sexuality. It was pretty foreign to me to discuss sex that openly with a group of strangers. I felt like a southern boy who, in the words of the singer Bob Seger, "had wandered too far from home." Yet, dealing with this issue, even though it felt forbidden, was exciting, especially since I knew we would all be getting naked together later, in the hot tubs.

The Esalen baths are known worldwide both as a place of beauty and experimentation. The natural hot tubs sat on the edge of huge cliffs overlooking the Pacific Ocean; their healing and revitalizing waters were well known to Big Sur's original residents, the ancient Esselen Indians, for whom the institute was named. I don't remember whether the experience was clothes-optional or not, but most people were naked. The water, with its natural minerals, was soothing and I was mesmerized by the sounds of the waves crashing against the rocks below. At night we could see the moon rising over the mountains from the tubs. People of both sexes and all ages and body types would be in the baths, and very soon the strangeness of being in public without clothes disappeared. Many celebrities visited Esalen, as well as teachers well-known nationally and internationally, so it was not uncommon to find myself soaking with people who were famous – or acted as if they were. The entire experience – the night sky, crashing sea, fresh air, hot mineral waters, and no clothes – was one of glorious simplicity.

I learned that presence lies not only in being physically present, but also the in quality of our attention. It invites us to be good listeners, whether listening to others or ourselves. This is one reason, I think, why so many people are replacing or complementing their medical doctors with alternative health practitioners. For me, being treated by the wonderful people who have helped me through my illness has been far more enjoyable than my visits to traditional practitioners, which in many instances felt like a necessity I had to endure.

I am extremely fond of many of the traditional doctors I've worked with, appreciate their incredible work and dedication and I highly value their contribution to my own and my family's well-being. But, because of their intense level of activity, I sometimes find they are only partially present with me. They may have patients in four or five rooms and often are running back and forth among them. In addition, they may be dictating notes, responding to their hospital patients, locating test results, writing prescriptions, and handling insurance issues simultaneously. It shocked me that after spending a week at a nationally known medical clinic having the most thorough of physical, when my coordinating doctor presented his findings, he mistook me for another patient and spent ten minutes talking to me about a neurological disease that was not my problem.

Small wonder that doctors may not even remember the name of the patient in front of them. The complexity of today's medical practice keeps simple attentiveness at bay. Many alternative practitioners enjoy the luxury to work with only one person at a time—or they have made a conscious decision to do so. They take down all the information themselves; they have no hospital practice or prescriptions to write. The benefits from their personal, undivided attention are a large part of the healing. People cherish being listened to. At a recent oncology conference, a presenting physician revealed that her former acupuncturist was the only person in a medical setting who had ever listened to every word she spoke. In all fairness, it is mostly the system rather than the individuals, and, in recent years, I am deeply indebted to traditional doctors for important and critical treatment to myself and family.

One place where I would see two cultures cross, one enviably simple and the other more complex, was at a bridge in North Florida running from Little Talbot Island to Amelia Island. At one time, the bridge was full of fishermen moving slowly, in Key West time, many of them old black folks talking the southern colloquial dialect. These people were never in a hurry. They fished, smoked a cigarette, drank a beer, maybe visited with a friend or two. Over time, Amelia Island became an upscale tennis and golf resort. The BMWs zipped back and forth over the bridge, usually driven by women with cell phones in hand and jewelry dangling from their wrists; they never seemed to notice the fishermen as they sped past. Was one of these two cultures more connected to God than the other? I decided the answer probably depended on the lens through which one looked, but my vote would go to the ones living simply and spaciously. Now there are two separate bridges to Amelia—one for fishing, one for traffic.

There is another place in which I annually see two cultures crossing. It's in Gainesville, Florida, at the opening football game of the University of Florida, which is attended by about 85,000 people – almost all wearing orange. I noticed through the years that the Hare Krishnas, mostly young Americans whose spiritual practice comes out of India and who have a large community in Gainesville, also arrived at the stadium in orange, the color of their particular "uniform." They approached with abandon, their bells jingling, tambourines shaking and heads bobbing as they chanted. In the last few years, the University marching band, more than a hundred strong, approached the stadium to the beat of their drums and horns at the very same time. These two groups marched through each other at some point, which was quite a sight. Recently, the two groups have seemed more appreciative and less disdainful of each other. The heart opens in its own time, regardless of the uniform covering it.

While I was writing this chapter I spoke to my daughter, Allison, who had just been admitted to the hospital because of premature labor with her second child. Her husband, Scott, had ordered certain medication to stop the contractions and it seemed to be working. She was an employment lawyer and was trying to finish up her last memorandum before breaking camp for the delivery. She was wired to the hospital monitors and told me that each time she thought about work, the monitors showed a contraction starting. She could actually see the powerful effect of the mind on the body; understanding that connection between the two allowed her to quiet the body by stilling her active mind.

I love the saying of Yogi Amrit Desai: "Whatever you believe, that is what you create and that is what you become." Two hundred years before, the great Hasidic rabbi, Rabbi Nachman of Breshlev, said essentially the same thing: "You are your thoughts." Dr. Deepak Chopra more recently has expanded that teaching observing that each thought we have immediately becomes a part of each cell in our body. He said it's likely that we're each related by DNA to the most famous and the most infamous people in history, from Joan of Ark to Benedict Arnold, if you just went back through enough generations and followed the genetic progression of the DNA. The point: we are all related, quite literally. This is a simple concept and reminds us of the simplicity that unites us.

Contrast this with white descendants of Thomas Jefferson, disavowing their relatedness to descendants of black slaves who claim to be in Jefferson's bloodline through their foremothers such as Sally

Hemings, who bore his children. This complex argument has divided Virginians and whites from blacks, again demonstrating that simplicity often unites while complexity divides.

I often use my beloved grandmother, Rose, as an example of simplicity. Rose lived until 1990 and died just before her ninety-ninth birthday. She was not doing the proactive things contemporary medicine tells us will prolong our lives. In fact, she simply laughed at the word "proactive." She didn't walk, meditate or watch her diet, which was characterized by indulgence rather than restraint. Each night at dinner, my mother would ask her, "Mother, would you like some seconds?" and Grandmother would respond, first with, "I don't think so," followed by, "Maybe just a little bit." Soon her plate would be full of another heaping helping of meat and potatoes. The same conversation would be repeated over dessert. Her "just a small piece of pie" was soon replaced by a large piece of pie which, in turn, would be followed by two heaping spoons of ice cream and "just a little" chocolate sauce to top it off. Between meals she exercised no greater restraint. Her pockets were always full of Snickers Bars, which she handed out to her grandchildren and great grandchildren "willy nilly," as she would say.

I have thought long and hard about the source of my grandmother's longevity. I believe it was rooted in the simple way she lived, together with a continuing enthusiasm for life-long learning. Her simplicity manifested in a variety of ways. She lived with my mother until age ninety-five and then in a nursing home for her last four years. After about a month of acclimation there, she quickly became an enthusiastic participant in the nursing home activities, particularly bingo and the religious services. She would telephone me after a successful night of bingo to report she had won a dollar and change and that it was available for gifts to her great grandchildren. She was usually the first seated, eagerly waiting for the game to begin.

Her continuing interest in education was reflected in her weekly attendance at the Sabbath service, at which she always sat in the center of the front row. The cantor who conducted the service would be just a few minutes into the morning lecture when her hand would go up. "Yes, Mrs. Schulhofer?" he would ask kindly. She, in turn, would ask a deep and fundamental question about life with her usual intensity. Her questions may have been as fundamental as "Is there a God?" and "Why are we here?" the same queries she might have made as a child. After a detour to answer one of her inquiries, the cantor would return to his planned lecture. Soon her hand would again shoot up with her next question. Her inquiries were profound and also spoke to the simplicity of reality.

Grandmother didn't really think about prolonging her life or why she had lived so long. She was a very healthy ninety-nine years old up until just two days before her passing. On the week before her death, she ventured out with my brother, Neal, to a local barbecue restaurant; within minutes, she downed an order of pork spare ribs and fries. I knew her to be sick only once and that was at age ninety-five, when she was diagnosed with colon cancer. She was operated on successfully and that was the last we heard about it. She really had the remarkable ability to put unpleasantness out of her mind.

A year before she died, I asked her to recount the bad things that had happened in her life. She said she really couldn't think of any. I reminded her of the colon cancer she'd had three years before, to which she replied, "Colon cancer? I don't remember that, but if you say I had it, I had it."

She hadn't suffered memory loss. Although she selectively forgot those parts of her life that had been unpleasant or painful, she was alert and articulate. Maybe this was a way she kept her life happy and simple, and which helped to account for her longevity. She never required any extra things or money or possessions. Whatever she had was sufficient. The only thing she really ever asked for was her family to be healthy. Ironically, she was so healthy that she outlived all three of her children; this was sad. I wonder if she might have lived several more years without the hardship of parental grief. When life becomes too complicated, I call her to mind as my role model, with loving remembrance.

Unbuttoned / Ken Fink

Chapter Fifteen

MEETING THE PROSPEROUS

"When one door of happiness closes, another opens;
but often we look so long at the closed door that we do
not see the one which has opened for us."
HELEN KELLER

Unbuttoned / Ken Fink

The question of who among us is prosperous is intriguing. In our society, prosperity is often measured by material possessions and degree of comfort. The belief is that if you have enough money, savings, cars, goods, retirement plan, etc., life will be safe and everything will be taken care of.

I come from what might be considered a moderately prosperous background. Yet my parents, who lived through the Great Depression, never felt fully secure. My mother told of a time when she broke a quart of milk and spent the next couple of hours crying over it. My father told of his father amassing wealth but then losing everything in the Depression. Although my parents were reasonably well-to-do, the fear of poverty or losing everything was deeply ingrained in us, and the repetition of certain stories helped form my beliefs about money and security. As a consequence, I have spent many hours counting my resources and worrying if I will have enough for the future. Some of the counting is practical and necessary, but some is based on fear and unreality.

On some semi-conscious level, I believed that when I reached a certain number, I would be safe. I'm not alone in this, from what I see in the media and particularly its business sections. When I'm more realistic, I see that my notion of safety is an illusion; a single event could roar through my life and take my health, money and life itself. The reverse is also true; another event could, in a moment, restore health and life, and manifest material wealth. I guess this is why so many people, including me, purchase lottery tickets. I remember the lines to enter the lottery seemed to go on forever when Florida's lottery began. Many people considered that, even with better than ten million-to-one odds stacked against them, the lottery promised the best and only way through their life's problems. Few have the tools to consider that their personal attitude and self-awareness might be a more valuable key.

However, the essence of prosperity is far broader than material accumulation alone. Prosperity begins as a state of mind in which one acts as if there is unlimited abundance; thus, there always will be enough. It also means that whatever goes to you will not in any way diminish what's left for me, since life's resources are infinite. Even the term "what's left" implies limitation.

Personally, I have not developed to the point where I can hold onto prosperity consciousness for very long, although I have been able to live it for short periods. My conditioning has made this state of mind a particularly difficult challenge for me, although for those few moments when I've experienced it, I felt remarkable free.

The way this plays out for me is that sometimes my personal identity becomes entangled with my net worth. If the stock market or real estate values soar and I feel better about my economic circumstances, I then also feel better about myself personally. As a result, when either of these values plummet, I become self-critical. I know that this is ridiculous, but the feelings still persist. I expect I've benefitted from being conscious of these self-deceptions – I tell myself with a grain of salt, "Look, there I go again" – but I look forward to the day when I'm able to value myself unconditionally regardless of the state of my estate. At such times I recollect the writings of Henry Miller, the great author of erotic literature and a prolific painter, who said he had reached the stage of life where he was free of most possessions and not dominated by his sex drive—making him the happiest he had ever been.

Through the years I've enjoyed listening to Yogi Amrit Desai speak about money. He says that when we come into money, we may lose more freedom than we gain since our mindset now wants both to hold on to it and to accumulate more. We get busy protecting what we have, he says, and then start to measure our worth by comparing what we have with what our neighbors have.

One of the most memorable statements I heard during my four years as an undergraduate at the Wharton School of Finance and Commerce was a quotation in a class on Russian economics. The Russian leader Vladimir Lenin stated that a man is typically satisfied with his house only until someone builds a larger one next door. In a similar vein, the comedian W.C. Fields, one of the greatest humorists of all time, was never satisfied with his incredible professional achievements because he always thought that Charlie Chaplin was funnier.

Soon after embarking on my spiritual journey, a counselor I met attempted to burst my bubble by criticizing everything I was doing. I made the case that even though I had gotten sick and was forced to give up the profession for which I had spent many years training, establishing a reputation, and developing expertise and clientele, there was value to my new path. I told him I was confident that the teachings and the personal lessons they evoked would make me valuable in a different and perhaps more useful way. He implied, pompously I thought, that nothing good could come from the things I was pursuing and accused me of "magical thinking." I left his office confused and a bit shaken.

The next day I heard on public radio a glowing presentation of Dr. Deepak Chopra's work, including his concept of magical thinking, which suggests that we can create new lives and new values if we allow ourselves to go beyond our usual, limited ways of thinking. So, which of the two definitions of magical thinking should I choose to live my life by? The one portraying me as a tragic figure grasping at straws and rationalizing the catastrophic end of a promising career, or the one that described me as a courageous pioneer forging a new trail when old plans went awry? Without hesitation, I chose the latter. That optimistic way of thinking is part of my new understanding and practice of prosperity consciousness.

I'd like to share what I've learned about prosperity from some of the people and their wealth – inner or outer – whose paths have crossed and impacted mine. Some of my close friends have substantial assets and prosperous mindsets, while others have prosperous mindsets and average or few assets. I've also known people with great wealth but very tight mindsets. I've noticed that, while obviously rich, these are the ones who never seem to derive any real joy or peace of mind from what they have.

One person, an acquaintance, recently purchased a multimillion-dollar showpiece of a home. When I was invited to a party there, I saw that, instead of enjoying his new home, he was preoccupied with the huge cost (several hundred thousand dollars) of an upgraded security system to protect this new asset. In contrast, I was once invited to the small room within a spiritual community where a friend lived. The invitation into his sacred space (his description) was very special for me. This man was devoted to his practices in every sense of the word. Not only was his room a temple, but to him so, too, was the lovely environment surrounding his modest home. He told me that, although he was only in his late twenties, he felt no need to leave that place for the rest of his life. Everything that he could possibly want was available there. He kept his door unlocked – no security system was needed to safeguard the little he had. Nor was he distracted by looking to acquire more or protect what he already had. With this prosperous mindset, he was almost always content. His belief was that he had all that he would ever need in the moment.

When I left the practice of law, one of my business associates I respected a great deal told me that his goal in life was to accumulate one million dollars so that he could be free. He described freedom as the ability to travel wherever he wanted and to be free to eat in any restaurant without being concerned with the cost. When I visited him several years later I reopened that earlier conversation. He told me, again, that he wanted to have enough resources to travel wherever he wanted and to dine at his pleasure at any restaurant in the world. He added that as soon as he reached three million dollars he would be free. (A moving target is hard to hit.) Sadly, he never fully enjoyed the actual extent of his material prosperity. It was always a goal he was going to reach in the future.

Another person with tremendous prosperity consciousness is acupuncturist Dr. Robert Chin. When I visited Dr. Chin, I didn't know for sure whether it was the needles or his healing presence that helped me. I told friends that the greeting he gave me at the door was by itself worth the trip across town. He would always ask how I was and after answering, I would then ask him how he was. His response was always the same: "I am wonderful, Mr. Fink, why would I choose to be anything else?" He dressed immaculately and was a physically strong and good-looking man. At one point in his early fifties, he bench pressed more than 400 pounds, more than most college football players can lift. He was also an eighth degree black belt in his particular form of karate. It was his motto that happiness is a choice and, at least in my presence, he lived that motto on a daily basis. I don't know what

Dr. Chin's financial status was, but he said to me years ago that he might retire one day and move to Hawaii. "I have accumulated little money for retirement, but I know that the Universe will take care of me." There is a great freedom in this awareness.

I once studied the soft martial art of Qigong with Dr. Chin. In that class he described a turning point in his life when, as a young man in Korea, some hothead had insulted him in a bar. He had the opportunity to break the man's neck, which he said he could have done easily, but instead he chose the path of peace and walked away. From that point on, he said, his peace of mind was his primary objective. I saw numerous occasions when he lived that motto. One day he returned from lunch three hours late. He told me that, although he regarded his peace of mind as his highest priority, he had been tested that day. "I dropped off my car at the automobile dealer and they promised to drive me directly to my office," he explained. "They knew I needed to be back by 1:00 because I had scheduled an afternoon full of people. Well, they filled their van with a number of other people and drove to outlying areas of the city first. It was 3:15 before I returned. I could have gotten very angry, but I didn't let this disrupt my day. Maintaining my peace of mind is a higher priority than any result my anger would have produced."

I thought about how angry I would have been in the same circumstance. In fact, just listening to the story made me angry. He showed me, however, that peace of mind is a choice, an inner dimension of prosperity that can be cultivated and practiced.

I do not have the kind of discipline I've seen in Dr. Chin and others, especially people from his culture and students of Eastern disciplines. In the West, we may exercise discipline over our money, weight, physical habits, lawns, the neatness of our homes, but we often allow our minds to run amuck. We are full of free-floating anxieties and worries. We allow fantasies of revenge, poverty, disaster and illness to consume our thoughts.

I once heard a speaker say, "I would never allow myself a thought that I didn't want to become." Similarly, the noted author, Dr. Deepak Chopra, has asserted that happy thoughts create endorphins, and the good health and euphoria that come with them, while unhappy thoughts create lack of ease, which leads to dis-ease.

The discipline that Dr. Chin learned in his training reigned over the mind as well as the body. This allowed him to focus his thoughts and actions so that his prosperity was always present. The ability to control the mind was used not only to keep negative thoughts at bay, but also to focus his mind to bring him joy and an embracing attitude. Once I asked him if he was going to follow through with a planned trip to Korea, his birthplace. He responded that he traveled every day with his mind. He said, "I can be in Korea one moment and a moment later in Hawaii. I can be with my friends and family in far away countries and even hear the distinctive sounds of the streets and revel in the smell of the local food."

Dr. Chin would experiment with gadgets and natural remedies as part of his practice. One time he had obtained some natural reindeer antler powder, which was considered a major booster of male sexual potency. I decided to try some even though it was expensive, and it worked like a charm. Maybe mind over matter, but I felt an extraordinary boost in my engine. I was in a state of constant excitement for about a week, although unfortunately my partner was busy and less available than usual. For the future I would need to remember the adage: "Success is when preparedness meets opportunity!"

Stanley is another friend whose life is a model of prosperity. At the time he and I met, he had left his plumbing practice in Massachusetts to come to energy school in Sedona with his wife, Carol, who was battling breast cancer and died the following year. While most of the students stayed in hotels, Stanley and Carol often camped out by the river. In the mornings, even when it had been raining, Stanley would talk ecstatically about the beauty of wherever he had spent the night. His home in Massachusetts was a modest caretaker's cottage but there was nothing modest about his surroundings – a beautiful New England tudor house and rolling lawns – which he treated with great care, as though they were his own. Through the years he has traveled to more places than most people could imagine. He filmed a spiritual school in the Pacific Islands; stayed at the ashram of Sai Baba, a revered Indian master; and hiked into the volcanoes of Hawaii, to mention just a few. He now lives in Montana, again in a caretaker's lodge. When he first moved there he described the place with so much enthusiasm that it made me want to get on a plane to visit instantly. At sixty, he has recently fallen in love again, and to listen to him tell about it, you would think you were talking to a teenager about his first love. Because of his enthusiastic openness, Stanley's world is truly his oyster.

My very good friend Gudni, an Icelander, is another model for what true prosperity looks like. Gudni and I met at Kripalu in the late 1980s. He was eleven years my junior, blonde, with little or no body fat, and Nordic. I was stocky, swarthy and Jewish. We couldn't have looked more different. Gudni was a mind-body trainer who trained a number of contestants for the Miss Iceland contests. We met in a program that revolved around a week-long raw juice fast, and we made a lasting connection that continues to deepen. Several months after that first meeting, he returned from Iceland and we both enrolled in a month-long Kripalu bodywork program.

Kripalu was a celibate community in the late 90s, so in the body-work class men worked only with men, and women worked only with women. Since there were only eight men out of the fifty participants, we came to know each other pretty well over the month of training, working on each other and hanging out together. Gudni had a fantastic sense of the body. He could read people just by looking at their body type, musculature and stance. From this, alone, he could often describe their history, their emotional issues, and their family backgrounds. It didn't take long before the teachers of the program asked Gudni to read the history and issues of those willing to receive this information. My body was locked and my gait was peculiar. It took no genius to discern this, but he helped me become more fluid and be more connected to my body. When we visit each other – he now lives in Los Angeles – I'm aware that he scans my body carefully during our first few minutes together, his eyes like a virtual MRI. This lets him know what's gone on since our last visit.

I prided myself on my connections, my ability to gain access to unavailable people or events, and being the first to make a new discovery. But I was no match for Gudni; he had usually gotten there first. If I found out that a noted astrologer from India was staying in a nearby cabin, by the time I showed up there I would learn that Gudni had just left. If I heard that an exciting concert was coming up, Gudni would already have front row tickets. Somehow he managed to do this with limited funds. This fascinated and impressed me.

Gudni took great care of his body and was highly sensitive to the impact of food on both his body and emotions. I've found that many people with a true prosperity consciousness give serious attention to their physical and energetic well-being. They do this not out of vanity, fear or guilt but, rather, because they really want to nourish and take care of themselves. They rarely diet but are attuned to the impact of foods and activities on their available energy. Typically, they will not feed the body more than it needs to accomplish its task. Since they manage their energy well, these are generally people with abundant physical energy.

Gudni had the ability and inclination to explore a variety of foods and body workouts to determine what worked for him at a given time. He worked out several times a day with clients, hiked with his dogs and his beautiful wife Gula, and worked out on his own. His choice of food over the years varied widely and it didn't always consist of what's classically considered "good food." One of his clients was a senior teacher at an institute internationally known for its nutrition and weight loss program. When Gudni walked into his training room at ten in the morning with a large bacon cheeseburger from Jack in the Box and a couple of orders of curly fires, the woman would cringe. But Gudni, because of his consciousness and level of breath and activity, could eat foods that others wouldn't dare and never be disturbed by them.

Most of the great saints and spiritual masters of the world, at one time or another, ate the coarsest of food in the poorest of surroundings with, or as, beggars. But because of their relationship to the whole of life, those foods nourished them well and they were often reported to glow. Conversely, I have observed people on strict health diets who, because of their lack of openness, seemed to gain little benefit from these regimens in spite of the discipline they maintained. Their gaze was often downward, and their bodies seemed contracted. Their choice of foods, like their choices in life, were often narrow. It appeared they suffered from a variety of food allergies and environmental sensitivities. I wondered whether the food caused the sensitivity or, more likely, the life conditioning caused the body to repel the food. I sensed that many of these people carried deep emotional wounds and that their physical struggles offered a doorway to a compassionate and healing relationship with themselves.

I had an informal dinner in Los Angeles with Gudni and his good friend, whom I'll call Cleo, one of the top body builders in Iceland. Cleo was returning to Iceland the next day for a competition. He busily ate pasta and salad, consistent with his strict regimen. Gudni had steak, potatoes and salad. Gudni cut a piece of the sirloin and placed it on the corner of Cleo's plate to taste because, "it is so delicious." Cleo actually jolted backward, his chair almost tumbling over in retreat. The effect was as though Arnold Schwarzeneggar had seen a mouse and jumped on a chair to get away from it. Gudni responded to his friend with gentle humor, "I promise you, Cleo, that the piece of steak can't hurt you, but your belief system can."

So much of the current information about food seems to create fear and confusion and takes much of the joy out of eating. For myself, since I'm prone to gain weight and have an inherited risk for heart disease from one side of my family, I was advised at an early age to limit meat, eggs and dairy products but eat all the fish and chicken I wanted. More recently, the well-respected book *Eat Right for Your Type* suggested I could eat beef and lamb but not chicken, since chicken doesn't digest well for those with my blood type. Recent articles have also reported that chicken is dangerous because of all the hormones they're fed, and that we should be careful of saltwater fish because they contain high levels of mercury.

Several years ago I was directed to eat soy instead of animal products. Then came a report which said that, in Japan, soy was used mostly as a condiment and not as a food staple, warning that the overuse of soy in this country could lead to health problems. The high protein diets

217

encourage us to keep away from carbohydrates, including fruit and bread, because of the insulin reaction, since insulin turns excess carbohydrates into fat. Conversely, low fat diets recommend that we eat fruit and whole grains, but urge us to stay away from animal products containing fats. One source advises us to eat protein shakes as a food substitute, while another says eat only real food. There is a book and radio program, *Dead Doctors Don't Lie*, that suggests the many benefits of the use of mega vitamins and supplements. Meanwhile, mainstream medicine warns that, since many vitamins and supplements are untested, their excess use or combination with other drugs could do us harm. (In reality, the pharmaceutical companies are trying to monopolize the vitamin and supplement market, and in the meantime, have lobbied the FDA to make such claims about independently produced supplements.) And then there's food contamination, e-coli bacteria, and the recently topical Mad Cow Disease and Avian Flu. Help!

I've found that those with prosperity consciousness seem less concerned than the rest of us with all of this hype. They eat with joy and moderation and are able to do so since they can easily assimilate and digest what they eat and eliminate what they don't need. I see this as a metaphor for how they live their lives.

To the extent that spiritual teachers or teachings disregard material wealth, they often cause unneeded problems. I don't subscribe to the belief that material wealth and God are incompatible. I believe God wants us all to experience abundance in all forms. Many seekers and some teachers have neglected to ground their spirituality and have forgotten that they're required to live within a physical body, and within a society that has certain requirements. They find themselves continually in trouble with creditors, licensing bureaus or tax collectors and consequently have difficulty maintaining their practices and their focus. While many of these people have very beautiful souls, I feel that some need a good shot of common sense spirituality.

In one instance, which admittedly may be extreme, I overheard a healer who I respected very much as a healer, advise his new girlfriend in regard to the substantial alimony payments she was receiving from her ex-husband. His advice was that she should spend her alimony right away so that it wouldn't be taxed. This was ridiculous advice; we all know that whether you spend the money or not, your income is still subject to income taxes. He either needed to ground his spirituality or take a good look at his ethics.

Money, of course, is a form of energy. It makes life easier in innumerable ways and may provide a sense of security. But sometimes an attachment to or preoccupation with money may lead us astray. Jesus said that it is harder for a wealthy man to get into heaven than a camel through the eye of a needle. This seems to me a bit exaggerated, but I'm not the director of admissions at heaven's gate!

I liked one teacher's way of meeting this. One of his students, at his graduation from healing school, said in all candor that it was his objective to make a vast amount of money, an unusual aspiration to reveal before a spiritual group. The teacher responded that making lots of money seemed to be in his soul and advised him to go ahead and become a millionaire if that was his current mission. But he also warned him not to get attached to the results or the money; it's the attachment that becomes the trap.

Many people of great wealth are now developing their consciousness and may become our spiritual barometers in the future. Oprah Winfrey, a fabulously wealthy woman, comes to mind. She devotes much of her show to raising consciousness. I marveled, at the beginning of her series on "spirit," how spellbound her audiences were when spiritual principles were presented. They seemed to be thirsting for new models to live by. In fact it may be that spirituality is the next hurdle for those who are materially comfortable, which is not surprising. Once they "have it all," it becomes possible to see what's really missing in their lives.

Michael Milken, the brilliant Wall Street entrepreneur who served almost two years behind bars on securities fraud charges, has established the largest private source of funding in the world for prostate cancer research. Jane Fonda is investing much of her energy and fortune in the eradication of world hunger. Richard Gere, a friend of the Dalai Lama, raises large sums for the people and monasteries of Tibet. These are just three of the many headliners who come to mind.

There are weekly meditation circles attended by Wall Street financiers in New York's financial district, daily sittings in the Pentagon for high level military personnel, and regular meditation and chanting gatherings for top international delegates to the UN. Among all the people I meet through my quite large network of spiritual seekers, healers and old souls, almost everyone has encountered major players in international business, show business, government and medicine in their workshops, spiritual retreats or healers' offices.

What's even more amazing is how many corporations are now bringing in consultants who work with their upper and middle management to stir creativity, open the heart, awaken intuition and develop a sense of interconnectedness. They understand that their companies can't truly prosper unless those who work for them are prospering, and money alone can't do that. The mystical poet David Whyte and visionary-futurist Jean Houston are just two of those who have been in great demand for the consciousness workshops they bring to corporate America. The very same qualities that would make CEOs and movie stars, alike, so charismatic and successful – their curiosity, ambition for themselves, vision and brilliance – are what would draw them to their own healing and awakening; they're much too smart to end their pursuit of happiness when their coffers are full. Because their leadership skills are so highly developed and their fields of influence so broad, those who explore the path of consciousness can, and undoubtedly will, help shape the new face of prosperity in our society.

Unbuttoned / Ken Fink

Chapter Sixteen

SOUL WARRIORS

"He comes to realize that the game is not against the foe,
but against himself. His little self. That yammering, fearful,
ever-resistant self that freezes, chokes, tops, nobbles, shanks,
skulls, duffs, flubs. This is the self we must defeat."
STEVEN PRESSFIELD, 'The Legend of Baggar Vance'

Unbuttoned / Ken Fink

*O*ur spiritual teachers are our most important warriors of this time. I call them "soul warriors." They are the harbingers of a new kind of human being – unified, heart-centered, bridging differences, respecting the ways of others. It is the sacred duty of each of us to move in this direction, away from separation and toward oneness. I consider doing this a necessity, not a choice. I look at it as the opportunity for each of us to help manifest what is best for everybody.

Modern-day soul warriors may be among our contemporary spiritual teachers. They come from the different religions, arts, sciences, politics or economic classes. Their common denominator is a spiritual orientation through which they're able to perceive the interconnectedness of life. More and more people who are successes in areas seemingly unrelated to consciousness have explored and embraced the spiritual dimension in their lives, which has broadened their contributions to their fields and the culture at large. They have done this by cultivating a wide and inclusive view of reality from which to apply their discipline. Albert Einstein was an excellent example of this new warrior. He experienced God and the infinite possibilities of the Universe as more pre-eminent than any of his scientific theories.

Our country is based on an adversarial system resulting from the constitution's mandate for checks and balances, which was designed to prevent any one group from running off with all the goods. My future vision tells me that someday in the not too distant future, this way of governing ourselves will be seen as primitive to historians and theologians. Although we are now stuck in this adversarial paradigm, just as though our feet are in mud, we have the capability of evolving to a more harmonious consciousness.

If one were to look with utterly no bias at what happens in and between our governments, institutions, families and primary relationships, what becomes obvious is that in all these contexts there are subtle and not-so-subtle forces continually in opposition to each other. It's as though there's a constant tug of war, with half in the system pulling one way on the rope and half pulling the other way. At some point, one of these two groups may muster more energy than the other, which gives them a victory or a "win." However, ninety-eight percent of the energy expended by both sides has been neutralized. Somehow, we consider this a success, despite the fact that only a minute fraction of the total energy expended moves the unit beyond where it started. People are willing to invest all their energy in these "wins," but the costs are enormous.

Consider our political system. Each side blames the other for over-spending and over-taxing, and takes credit for every budget surplus and any decision considered positive. Each party denigrates the other and discredits its leadership, its morals and its intent. President Clinton's impeachment is a perfect example. The country came to a virtual standstill while the two parties battled it out. In that process, President Clinton was scorched—but so were Newt Gingrich, the Republican speaker of the House, and Henry Hyde, head of the Senate Judiciary Committee, who were besmirched with similar allegations and revelations of past affairs. Charges sailed back and forth. Little progress was made on truly important issues. By the end of the impeachment proceedings, only a few votes had changed in the House, and none had changed in the Senate. This was a tremendous expenditure of energy that paralyzed almost everything else happening in the country. During this period, while our leaders were distracted trying to obtain a no-win victory through weeks of bitter fighting, India set off an atomic bomb, which caught Congress and everyone else by complete surprise. As Bagger tells Junah, his pupil, in *The Legend of Bagger Vance*, " 'Victory' and 'defeat'...I'm sick to death of them, and of men contending as if there was any difference between them! What good ever came of human beings facing one another in conflict?"

At some point, there must be an ability to move forward in a way that benefits all. Imagine if we all pulled our oars in the same direction at the same time, and we consciously chose to proceed this way without the threat of cosmic disaster to persuade us to work together.

The same adversarial context is reflected in our legal system. On the criminal side, a part of the population is unable to make it through the system, so they look for a way to circumvent it. Maintaining our prison system through both public and private funding is now one of the largest businesses in the country. Even if the circumventers are caught, a certain number escape through legal loopholes, or because there aren't enough jails to house them. Others end up serving only minimum time. Once released, they likely repeat their offenses, including violent acts, and even escalate sociopathic behavior in response to the harshness of the system that rejected or could never find a place for them. There are now more than two million men and women languishing in jails and prisons in this country– most of them victims of abuse by their families, environment and society long before they victimized themselves primarily through substance abuse, and others, primarily with their understandable rage. People who feel they've been marginalized by the rest of us and have no way to enter

society as free, self-determining participants become bitter and antag-
onistic. They are the most obvious casualties of a division into which
we have placed "them" and "us," the "haves" and the "have-nots."

This dynamic is not limited to the obvious outcasts. It shows up
everywhere: between men and women, adults and children, the insiders
versus the outsiders in schools, offices and on playing fields, and against
people of color, gay people, those handicapped physically, mentally or
emotionally, and wherever there's a caste system of any kind.

Our spiritual teachers try to bring us together to show us that there
really is no separation. They urge us to share the aspects of our lives we
have in common, which tend to connect us and engender compassion
for suffering. They demonstrate that we can be present with the
disparate parts of ourselves, those parts that we have denied, both as
individuals and within the social aggregate. In place of conflict and war
they offer ways of conflict resolution that seek win-win solutions in
which all parties benefit. And they understand that the greatest healing
comes when people are willing to open to another's experience, figura-
tively standing in the enemy's shoes.

A recent example, which I mentioned previously, is Marianne
Williamson's work to heal the pain between peoples. At the gathering
I attended, white Americans apologized to Native Americans for the
injustices committed toward them through the years. They acknowledged that the actions of their government and people were wrong. By
the end of the evening, the tension between the two groups had
dissolved and everyone felt closer. This is the opposite of adversarial
action. We all pulled in the same direction. We had a common intention for healing and so that's what we experienced. If we're willing to
emphasize our human relatedness, to stretch ourselves, we can find
essential similarities between descendants from Lithuania, part of my

heritage, and the Apaches of the Southwest. Is the experience of imprisonment for Geronimo and his followers essentially different from the internment of minorities in Nazi concentration camps?

I recently attended a good friend's bachelor party, which was held at a beautiful private club around a large conference table. I probably didn't realize that I had had too much to drink on an empty stomach when I got up to give my toast. After praising the groom and telling a few jokes, I then expressed genuine love for all those gathered for the dinner—a cross-section of different nationalities, levels of wealth and social classes. I expressed myself in a sort of gushy, non-masculine way. A few of the men joked good-naturedly about my presentation throughout the weekend that followed, but I was pleased with myself for two reasons. First, behind all the bravado, I truly held deep heart-felt feelings and hopes of love and togetherness for this gathering of men and their families. Secondly, I was able to speak that vision and intention in front of an unlikely audience. The martinis may have oiled the system, but the words were exactly what the system was feeling.

I've mentioned many of the heroes with whom I've had contact through this long journey. Most of them work primarily with conscious-ness or healing, since these have been the people I've come to know in this recent part of my life. There are also, of course, many heroic people and actions who emerged from formal religion, medicine, the arts, and the sciences. Mother Teresa is an example. Through her work toward eliminating poverty and hunger in the world, she had an enor-mous impact and also inspired millions. Doctors Without Borders brings compassion and medicine to remote parts of the world that are in dire need of such help. There are thousands of other people and groups similarly dedicated. Among those who have touched and spoken to my deeper self are John Denver, Magic Johnson, Shirley MacLaine,

Ben Cohen of Ben and Jerry's Ice Cream, Ram Dass, Dr. Deepak Chopra, Alan Cohen, John Lennon, Paul McCartney, Bono, Oprah Winfrey, Maya Angelou, Billie Jean King, Dr. David Hawkins, The Innocence Project and Habitat for Humanity.

True leaders always recognize our interrelatedness. Whether they are labeled traditional or alternative, they recognize that AIDS is not someone else's problem; it's ours. Mad cow disease is not a British problem; it's a world problem, as evidenced by its detection in the U.S. in 2003. Even before September 11, they recognized that terrorism was a problem not just in the Mideast and Europe; it was a world problem. Soul warriors see the interconnectedness of all people and issues and do not fragment human problems into "our" problems and "your" problems.

It's a particularly tough task for men who are spiritual teachers and healers, at least in this country. Not only are they considered outside the cultural mainstream, but there are some who also consider these hearty, sensitive souls outside the mainstream of masculinity. At a gathering of male healers several years ago, I heard one man say that when he started explaining to people at a social gathering what his work was, the group suddenly become silent. He lived beyond their belief system and that disturbed them.

I love sports and have followed them intensely for years. I'm familiar with records, with top teams in a given year, with specific athletes, and I appreciate fantastic feats of athleticism. Yet I balk when eighteen and nineteen-year-olds are idolized, made into national heroes and given $75 million contracts. J.C. Watts knows more about life after his six terms in the U.S. House of Representatives than he did as a star quarterback for the University of Oklahoma. Alan Page is far wiser as a Minnesota Supreme Court justice than when he ran down quarterbacks as a part of the Minnesota Vikings' fabled "Purple People Eaters." Payne Stewart learned far more about life in the mid-1990s while suffering through the worst slump of his PGA golf career and watching his best friend, fellow golfer Paul Azinger, battle for his life from cancer. He had a spiritual awakening, became a much more sensitive and happy husband, father and man, grew to become one of the most-loved players on the tour, and captured the 1999 U.S. Open in dramatic fashion to hit the high mark of his career at age 42. He died in a plane crash the week before he would've been named Ryder Cup captain—to him, the ultimate achievement in golf because the Ryder Cup was about teamwork, attaining a goal as a unit. Four thousand people attended his funeral, led by Paul Azinger, Tiger Woods and the entire PGA Tour, where the pastor, family and friends conveyed the theme of Payne as a hero—the Joseph Campbell conception of hero, not the 18-year-old sports whiz. That's making an impact as a spiritual warrior.

Sadly, we often don't acknowledge many of the spiritual warriors who are blazing the trails for humanity and are forging the direction for the health and well-being of our descendants. Some of the people and groups with whom I've spent time might be seen as at odds with each other. But the more I experience, the fewer differences I see between groups that may be considered disparate. Sometimes two seemingly quite opposite forces are no different than a game which has one team wearing orange and the other wearing green, with their jerseys easily interchangeable. I once attended services of several different religions over a short period of time and was most aware of their similarities. For example, each denomination had a reverent understanding of the lighting of candles. Each showed a reverence for the departed and concern for the sick and the disadvantaged. When I became aware of this, I found I could open to the higher experience each, in its own way, offered.

I believe that all paths which carry the intention to lead to God, spirit, or whatever one names that higher power, can help people find their way there. This is particularly true if right intent is coupled with commitment, love and forgiveness. We never know what the next turn holds for us or for the collective, but with a higher awareness of reality, we can make a difference. It is my hope that we can each locate the soul warrior within ourselves.

Most soul warriors, actually, are ordinary people like you and me. One who comes to mind is Judy, who is a very close friend from my years at the Jaffe School. She was at a workshop in Europe when she learned that swastikas had recently been painted on a nearby building. Judy has a huge heart and plenty of courage and will not let an injustice go by silently. Being the soul warrior that she is, she got a bucket of paint and painted the swastikas into hearts, enjoying herself throughout the process. By this action she became a spiritual teacher for all of us, transforming an act of hate into an act of love.

The job of the spiritual teacher is to lead. Through our life experiences, all of us have a spiritual teacher within us. This standing should not be reserved for a select few. It is the part of us that heals rather than hurts, that unifies rather than divides. It sees the beauty in all things and knows that what doesn't look beautiful is also within each of us and an intrinsic part of the human condition. There are many ways to reach that place that serves us all well. This learning was a gift of my journey and I'm grateful for the personal evolution that allowed me to receive it.

Chapter Seventeen

COMING HOME

"There is nothing like returning to a place that remains unchanged
to find the ways in which you yourself have altered."
NELSON MANDELA, 'Long Walk to Freedom'

Unbuttoned / Ken Fink

here is no end to the journey of transformation. Once we become conscious of ourselves as evolving beings, change and awareness become part of our ongoing process. At any given moment, each of us sees only a small part of reality. There is much more unknown than known, more unrealized than realized. In all experiences, it's the process that's important; as Harry Chapin sang, "it is the going and not the getting there."

Women often want their men to change. They ask their partners to become more sensitive, more communicative and more attentive. For these changes to be implemented and long-lasting, a change beyond simple behavior is required; it involves the very makeup of their soul. Men benefit from such changes and, to the extent that I've changed in regard to what women generally prefer, it's served me well.

When men make the changes that are requested, there are still a couple of surprises for both genders. By and large, men may find that, surprisingly, they are now less attractive to the opposite sex. They are expected to make major shifts in themselves without any deterioration in their earning power or their ability to protect, defend and provide security to their women. In my observation, these other qualities are the ones most valued by women, and greater sensitivity and conscious-ness are desired as an addition to the traditional core demands. In *The Myth of Male Power*, Warren Farrell indicated that one of the main reasons a woman picks a man is to have the choice of whether or not to work. He wrote that when one person in a couple removed themselves from the work force, it was almost always the woman. While this is still the tendency, it is less true today.

And so, to the women reading this: If you want your man to become more accessible, more heart-centered and more open, it may happen at a price. He'll probably let go of the driven behavior which, among other things, has helped provide you with a high standard of living. You may need to be willing to take up the slack with those particular responsibilities he took on as a function of his male conditioning or intensity.

The changes that men and women want from each other is not really what this book is about. Mostly I have addressed deep soul changes that are brought on from within, not forced in order to please a partner, although relationship issues can certainly be the instigating factor in a transformational change.

My own process has been worthwhile and I am forever grateful for it. Some of it was painful, much was uncomfortable, particularly in the early stages, and all of it was challenging. Without the traumas at the beginning, I never would have sought change to this degree and would probably have spent the majority of my life in the same setting, as do many people who grow up in my community. This is comfortable for many and preferred by others. However, my soul yearned for the changes and the challenges that came with them. Opportunities for change are a gift to be welcomed.

The elements of my life that I released had provided a measure of safety, security and respect, and in many ways defined who I was. A new identity was now called for. Gone was the comfort of fitting into the mainstream, acceptance by society at large, and a belief that I knew where I was going. Plan A, formulated in my youth, was now out the window.

I found much more of value than what I had surrendered. These were certain missing parts of myself. I have developed a strong spiritual side and am often able to open my heart to touch into the delicate and sensitive parts of the Universe. Sometimes when I speak I'm moved to tears or more frequently unable to speak until I regain my composure. These emotions were not accessible to me as a corporate lawyer. The feelings were buried somewhere, but I was unable to access them. Too many obstacles and too much conditioning stood in the way.

Previously, I had been able to deliver a planned speech and was quite facile and very comfortable talking at length before a large audience. Speaking from the heart is different. It may require standing before your audience not knowing where you are going or what will emerge and allowing the inner self to dictate the words. I also feel that I gained something more to offer to my companions, children and friends through the benefits of my experiences. I have a larger life to share, a life that has moved beyond the community and the groups with whom I had grown up. But I've needed to be patient and wait until these people who bridge both my distant and recent past have the listening capability to take in something that's new and different.

In unbuttoning and coming home, I've dealt with the parts of myself that were missing or from which I'd disassociated. I previously had no creative outlet, as true creativity had not been considered of value. I had taken the perfunctory piano lessons growing up, but this was approached more as a type of schooling than as creative expression. Through my process of return, I've taken up writing, along with energetic healing and African drumming.

While everything has changed on one level, on another everything remains the same. I don't pretend to be an enlightened being, although I feel I'm capable of more awareness and compassion. I physically look about the same, except for the added years and some added weight that seems to find me wherever I go. I notice that I continue to have the same tendencies of leading with my head, getting too busy or trying to push through instead of allowing. I still have an inclination to be reactive instead of responsive and at times fail to see the forest for the trees. But there is a different consciousness available, which offers me a choice to deal differently than in a habitual way with each of these situations. In other ways I remain stuck and don't seem able to use tools of higher consciousness.

Not surprisingly, I've found that our spiritual teachers are all subject to human frailty and most suffer from one or more of such human frailties as large egos, greed, infidelity, untruthfulness, projection, blindness to their own faults and discriminatory views. Some also seem quite ordinary when not on stage or leading a ceremony. Several I can think of could easily be mistaken for the cook in a diner. The healers and spiritual teachers I've met, however, tend to reflect upon their own shortcomings to a greater extent than the average person.

Although my physical symptoms are less frequent or at times infrequent, I must be constantly careful or they will reappear. When a symptom does show up, I must cut back substantially and immediately go into a resting mode. Gone is the A personality, along with the endurance to sustain it. But in taking a lot of time for myself, I'm able to find the balance to operate in the world.

On the surface I may appear just as I had been to people who haven't seem me for years. Maybe this is a reason why one can't be a prophet in his own land. People confine themselves to the identity they've formed of me over the course of many years. There may also be a tendency on my part to react in historical and habitual ways with those from the past, even though I know that the possibility of showing up differently holds the greater potential for both of us.

Recently, I ran into an old acquaintance who had taken a job that had required him to travel to Russia at least thirty times. I had the ridiculous thought, "He doesn't look like someone who has traveled to Russia thirty times," expecting the new experiences to actually show on his face or mannerisms.

I often use visual images of people I've met when I'm in need of some quality of life I observed in them. This helps me introduce or reinforce this quality in myself and is actually a joyful process. If I need to slow down my eating, I conjure up the image of Anup, a friend from Kripalu, sitting at a long table by himself, his jaw thrust out as he chews each bite over and over again as a practice of conscious eating. If I'm in supportive but strange surroundings, I remember the massage therapist who told me on a subfreezing day in Massachusetts that he had once lived at the ocean in San Diego, in an exquisite house and with a great climate, but his life worked better in this small room with no windows. When I get angry, I visualize Jason Shulman telling his class that he had snapped at a stranger in a donut line when he knew better, and how important it was that he forgive himself and move on.

During this time I also learned several skills I didn't have before. One was West African drumming, something that had always raised my energy and enthusiasm. I use the drum to help recapture some of the energy I had lost during an earlier period of total fatigue. I've also become a fan of foreign movies and one day might try my hand at a screenplay. It took a willingness to slow down to be able to sit through a movie with subtitles and savor a story which others might call a "chick flick" and which is built on nuance and subtlety. At the same time, I continue to love the action movies with Robert DeNiro, Clint Eastwood, Bruce Willis and Denzel Washington.

I've learned a great deal about alternative health and met many alternative practitioners, who now are among my best friends and contacts. I have gained some knowledge of foods, supplements and understandings about health, which now form an integral part of my well-being.

Because of the widening of my interests, I've been able to introduce different ideas to my children, friends and people I meet along the way. My son has co-written a fantastic screenplay with his good friend Jay, and both of my daughters have at one time or another taken up drumming made forays into alternative health modalities and also talk of writing screenplays in the future.

I'm more in touch with my life on the inner planes. This inner life connects with my interest in subtle energies and seeing how life expresses through different planes of consciousness. It has also drawn knowing, which I now trust as my surest guide to what's right for me. My changes also include a new relationship with God and appreciation of the divine on a heartfelt level. This relationship transcends any requirement for attendance at religious services so that I'm acceptable to a particular community of people, many of whom seem to perfunctorily participate in their religion but with little connection or reverence for the divine.

I've spent time with great teachers and healers of personal and spiritual growth, and call many of them my friends. I'm deeply moved when I think about them, their courage and pioneering spirit, and the contributions they are making to the world. Even more important, I've learned to be a healer. This includes the willingness to listen, to be compassionate, and to use my heart and instincts for understanding.

I'm also aware that in each of these healing encounters, I am part of the process. It's never just about the other person; it is about me, as well, although I may lose sight of that momentarily. I can now observe my reactions with a clear awareness and try to stay attuned to whatever strong negative responses to others arise in me. I see that my reactions to what's outside of me are mostly reflections of myself.

The coming home process has also brought up issues of the body, including the the terror of feeling my life force slip away and of not knowing what is happening to my body. By necessity, I have dealt with questions about my existence and issues around my mortality.

In spite of all the growth and deepening, and my sometimes gushy way of talking about these things, I will be the first to admit that I can, at times, still be a complete ass. I have a quick temper and harbor resentments, overindulge, wallow around in a funk, and am subject to all the human weaknesses that I had before. When I recently asked my children to name my faults, they told me they thought I was manipulative and overly persistent. I also know that I can easily become self-absorbed. But I'm now able to see these tendencies with more awareness and compassion. The tremendous value of being awake to myself is that it gives me the choice to stop and temper my reactions and then look for the underlying issue that got triggered in me. I believe that the more aware we are, the more responsibility we bear, and so an inappropriate response on my part now weighs heavier than when I knew less.

I understand that the transformational process is continuous, that there may be peaks and valleys, but once someone opens to it, they usually are guided by it throughout their lives. I expect this to be true for myself, as well, and look to the Universe for guidance in pointing to my future path. This process is a self-correcting mechanism. Life will present the circumstances necessary to challenge what is out of balance or what needs correction so that we all can grow into wholeness.

My journey has taken me from the boardroom to the ashram and settled in a place that includes both. There is no good or bad, just different circumstances to live with and the different opportunities and challenges they provide. I believe that I'm now more whole and harmonious and, from that place, experience and express life more fully.

Life is very intense at times and, at other times, it plateaus and becomes calm for a period. But there's now a difference for me between intensity and chaos. In a polarity session at Kripalu many years earlier, the practitioner pointed out to me that I had always identified with chaos. "You are the tranquility, as well," he said. "Identify with that." And so I see that I have a choice, even in times of intensity, to cultivate calmness. I've also learned that intense periods often offer an opportunity to reconnect with parts of myself that have been rejected or simply were never allowed to develop. When I become unbalanced, my life continues for awhile in that state and then something pushes me to confront that part of myself which needs to be present for balance to be restored. The more essential the missing part, the more intense the push to discover and reunite with that which will make me whole and complete. One often sees this when people become seriously ill; they're forced to dramatically reorder their lives.

During the period I practiced law, I was missing my feminine and creative aspects. I was once told that all the belief systems in my family of origin were masculine. This is probably one reason my personal journey pushed me toward women teachers and teachings concerned with healing, nurturing, listening and matters of the heart.

If I had been missing masculine or competitive aspects, then when life became intolerable without that missing part I would have been pushed toward people or events of a traditional masculine or competitive nature. The transformational process offers a self-balancing mechanism. If I stay open to the process, the call for my attention and growth can be heard and met with grace.

I personally needed the experience I was given so that I could come back into a balance I hadn't known since childhood. This brought me to a coming home to myself, to the person I was born to be. My journey reminds me of the archetypal adventure the mythological Ulysses took as described in *The Odyssey*. He left home as a young man to fight the Trojan War, which then brought him to a series of encounters within the vast unknown. He met many obstacles and diversions along that path. These included seduction by the Sirens, an enchanting and mesmerizing group of women, among whom he fell into a reverie for many years. He did battle with the monstrous one-eyed Cyclops and then had to deal with Neptune, God of the Sea, who took vengeance on him because of injustices Ulysses had done to his daughter. By the time he returned home twenty years later, he was unrecognizable except by his old dog Argus. He was a different man, changed and matured by all he'd encountered.

Once we come home to ourselves, we have usually changed a great deal. Some of what was lacking probably has been found, and so we're now more complete. It's also a little more difficult to knock us off our balance, as we're now more grounded physically and emotionally. We quite likely have acknowledged the wisdom of the Universe in giving us this experience, although it probably had its share of pain and difficulty, particularly at the outset.

When we've made a stronger connection with God or a higher power, the world seems to us less capricious, perhaps kinder and more intentional. How we spend our time now doesn't matter that much.

Typically, we are able to perform whatever is before us with more inspiration and purposefulness, knowing that we are contributing to the larger picture. This was the way it happened, in the story told earlier, with the banker who after his journey to the top of the mountain to discover the meaning of life returned to the job he had held some twenty years before. We also know that life may call on us again and again to do a piece of transformation, usually when we least expect it and regardless of age. Many people do their most important work as they are dying.

I have less of a plan now than I've had in the past. My prior plan was blown out of the water, so I now give less attention to what I think should come next. Maybe this is because I'm older or maybe I've realized that, while I'm busy making plans, life comes along with its own agenda for me. I try to stay attuned to what comes looking for me, calling my name with an offer that's exactly perfect for me at that moment. I have pushed hard on a lot of doors that haven't budged and have learned that when the situation is right, and my intention is clear, the door will open.

As to where my attention will be directed in the future, I know it will be far different from what the nay-sayers expect. As Helen Keller said, "No pessimist ever discovered the secret of the stars or sailed to an uncharted land, or opened a new doorway for the human spirit."

ACKNOWLEDGMENTS

Unbuttoned / Ken Fink

.

I wish to express my heartfelt thanks to the following: Bob Yehling for resonating with my journey and for his editing and marketing skills and connections; Marjorie Bair for her professionalism and considerable skills in the book's development and for understanding my journey, which provided immeasurable support and comfort;

Carol Hamilton for her help with the early drafts;

Camillus Brown for her typing skills and fine eye, which helped right things when they went awry;

Jamie Saloff for her skills in formatting and production and for her encouragement mixed with humor gently urging me to move things along;

and to Denise for her artistic designs, her technical computer skills and for putting up with my uneven temperament when the words didn't come as planned, and also for her help in keeping the computer humming.

My thanks and appreciation for inspiration and support to: my good friends Gundi, Fred, Lucy, and Brian, for reminding me that I had something important to say;

my children Julie, Allison and Ben and their partners Jeff, Scott and Samantha for presenting real life situations for me to try out my new learning;

Nancy Aronie for the week of writing in her home and for recognizing that I had something special to offer;

Gabrielle Rico for her encouragement and contacts; and

Ronda and Sandy for their continuous encouragement and heart-felt exchanges and their continuious challenges to move my work along with occassional kalua coffees to loosen the inhibitions in the PaPa Hemingway mold at our weekly coffee house writing sessions;

and to Doreen Sabina for her abundant enthusiasm and persever-ance in connection with getting this book out to the public;

and to the residents of Atlantic Beach, Florida for creating the type of community in which we all want to live.

I offer a special acknowledgment to the spiritual and motivational teachers whose paths I have had the privilege to cross, and who continue to blaze a trail into the future filled with love, light and higher consciousness.

Printed in the United States
50840LVS00005B/1-102